Public Participation, Scien and Society

The field of public participation is developing fast, with phenomena such as citizen science and crowdsourcing extending the resource base of research, stimulating innovation and making science more accessible to the general population.

Promoting public participation means giving more weight to citizens and civil society actors in the definition of research needs and in the implementation of research and innovation. As yet, there is limited understanding of the implications of widespread use of public participation and as a result, there is a risk that it will become a burden for research and an obstacle to bridging the gap between research and society. This volume presents the findings of a three-year international study on innovative public participation. The resulting work studies the characteristics and trends of innovative public participation through a global sample of 38 case studies. It provides theoretical generalisations on the dynamics of public participation, suggestions for an evaluation framework and clear empirical examples of how public participation works in practice. Illustrated by best practice cases, the authors identify characteristics which contribute to successful public participation.

The book is aimed primarily at scholars and practitioners of public participation, as well as research managers, policy makers and business actors interested in related issues. There is also a secondary market for students and scholars of European governance studies, sociology and political sciences.

Mikko Rask is Adjunct Professor and Principal Investigator at the University of Helsinki, Finland.

Saulė Mačiukaitė-Žvinienė is Senior Researcher at Vilnius University, Lithuania, and a Policy Adviser for the Republic of Lithuania on innovation, research and education, and an Expert of the European Commission.

Loreta Tauginienė is Researcher in Ethics Management and Head of the Academic Ethics Centre at Mykolas Romeris University, Lithuania.

Vytautas Dikčius is Professor at Vilnius University Business School (VU BS), Lithuania.

Kaisa Matschoss is Adjunct Professor at the University of Eastern Finland and works as a university researcher at the Consumer Society Research Centre at the University of Helsinki, Finland.

Timo Aarrevaara is Professor of Public Management at the University of Lapland, Finland.

Luciano d'Andrea is a sociologist who has been working on issues at the crossroads of social dynamics, economics and technological transformation.

Public Participation, Science and Society

Tools for Dynamic and Responsible Governance of Research and Innovation

Mikko Rask, Saulė Mačiukaitė-Žvinienė, Loreta Tauginienė, Vytautas Dikčius, Kaisa Matschoss, Timo Aarrevaara and Luciano d'Andrea

Routledge
Taylor & Francis Group

LONDON AND NEW YORK

First published 2018
by Routledge
2 Park Square, Milton Park, Abingdon, Oxon OX14 4RN

and by Routledge
711 Third Avenue, New York, NY 10017

Routledge is an imprint of the Taylor & Francis Group, an informa business

British Library Cataloguing-in-Publication Data
A catalogue record for this book is available from the British Library

Library of Congress Cataloging-in-Publication Data
A catalog record for this book has been requested

ISBN: 978-1-138-57495-3 (hbk)
ISBN: 978-0-367-89102-2 (pbk)

Typeset in Times New Roman by
Apex CoVantage, LLC

Contents

vi *Contents*

Figures

Tables

Boxes

Contributors

Mikko Rask is Adjunct Professor and Principal Investigator at the University of Helsinki. He is also the coordinator of the University of Helsinki Demola. He has had 20 years of experience as a researcher in several international and national level projects on citizen deliberation, technology assessment, foresight, research and innovation policy, and sustainability issues. He has published widely on these themes in several international books and journals, taught courses and lectured at several universities. He was also the co-founder and first chair of the Finnish Institute for Deliberative Democracy. He recently coordinated the EU-funded PE2020 project.

Saulė Mačiukaitė-Žvinienė has a doctoral degree of social sciences and is an active member of academia and society. She is Senior Researcher at Vilnius University, a Policy Adviser for the President of the Republic of Lithuania on innovation, research and education, and an Expert of the European Commission. She is the author of number of scholarly publications in peer-reviewed journals and studies on policy evaluation, deliberative democracy, science and innovation policy and governance. She has participated in numerous international projects, activities of the United Nations, European University Association and the European Commission as a national correspondent.

Loreta Tauginienė is Researcher in Ethics Management and a Head of Academic Ethics Centre at Mykolas Romeris University, Lithuania. Her research interests are university social responsibility, academic research integrity, public engagement, citizen science and responsible research and innovation. She is a co-author of four books, and has published over ten scientific articles. She is a member of the Board of European Network for Academic Integrity.

Vytautas Dikčius is Professor at Vilnius University Business School (VU BS), Lithuania. He is a member of MITA (Agency for Science,

Innovation and Technology) Council of Social Science, Lithuania. Also, he works as an expert of Research Council of Lithuania and participates in numerous types of evaluation. He has published more than 35 articles in both national and international peer-reviewed journals, has issued two textbooks about marketing research. He acquired his knowledge of innovation and business research during his professorship at the universities and while working as a project manager, consultant and director of several private sector companies. His areas of research interest include innovations, marketing communications and consumers' behaviour in different cultures.

Kaisa Matschoss, Adjunct Professor at the University of Eastern Finland, works as a university researcher at the Consumer Society Research Centre at the University of Helsinki. Her research interests lie in the fields of sustainable energy, innovations and public engagement. She has explored customer needs for smart grid applications, customer interest in smart energy efficiency services and energy efficiency retrofits in existing building stock as well as public and stakeholder engagement in sustainable innovations. She is studying the sustainability transition of the energy sector, the role of intermediary organisations in energy transition, experimentation and bottom-up transformation of energy use in households and communities across Europe.

Timo Aarrevaara is Professor of Public Management at the University of Lapland, and has professional experience in public administration as well as in research and teaching. He has participated in and conducted several evaluation and auditing projects, and has acted as the principal investigator of the ProSoc research team and in a number of projects, including the PE2020 work package for pilot initiatives, and the Changing Academic Profession (CAP) survey in Finland.

Luciano d'Andrea, a sociologist, has been working on issues at the crossroads of social dynamics, economics and technological transformation. He has worked as a senior research consultant in developing and emerging countries throughout Africa, Asia and the Americas. He has authored many articles and books. He is the editor of the Italian journal *Conoscenza & Innovazione* (*Knowledge & Innovation*). He has worked on several EC-funded projects, including SS-ERC, BESSE and CONSENT. He edited, with Wiebe E. Bijker, the *Handbook on the Socialisation of Scientific and Technological Research*. Recently he edited, with Wiebe E. Bijker and Giovanni Caiati, a handbook on *Knowledge Brokerage for Environmentally Sustainable Sanitation*.

Foreword

European research policy strives to address articulated concerns, some of the most pressing being the paucity of economic growth in Europe, youth unemployment and common societal challenges such as health issues, environmental challenges and sustainability. In these deliberations it is vital to keep in mind the concept of European added value. It is not a zero-sum game with each constituent nation competing for comparative advantage; rather it is a group of nations with strong common values striving for enhancement of society as a whole. This approach has led to shared roadmaps for research and innovation activities as well as to strong collaboration on major research infrastructures with defined rules for common access.

Responsible research and innovation (RRI) is one of the current policy frameworks for the development of more advanced forms of science governance in the European research area. RRI aims at improved dialogues and mobility between sectors of the society, including public institutions, enterprises, research and technology actors, citizens and civil society at large. Dynamic interactions across institutions and actors can contribute to better quality of research, as more people are able to mobilise their experience and expertise in collective problem-solving efforts.

Researchers can also expect to increase the impact of the efforts by observing pathways to application not otherwise evident.

Public engagement has been an important element in implementing responsible research and innovation policies. Several new approaches, such as citizen science, crowdsourcing, participatory budgeting, deliberative citizen panels, citizen and stakeholder based foresight processes and so forth have rapidly emerged in the European research landscape. Yet, while such approaches are becoming commonplace and public money is increasingly being spent on them, it has remained unclear how to evaluate the appropriateness, efficacy and impacts of such processes.

This book is a timely contribution to the discussion on the role of public engagement in research and innovation activity. In giving an analysis of the trends and characteristics of innovative public engagement, it can serve as a useful guide to those planning such activities. Perhaps most importantly, the book develops a synthetic model for evaluating the impacts and benefits of public engagement. The contributors are to be congratulated on this outcome, and I sincerely hope that the work on cataloguing and compiling lessons learned can be continued.

Martin Hynes,
President, European Science Foundation

Preface

Public participation in science has become a booming field of research, practice and experimentation. New models of participation, including citizen science, science parliaments, mock trials, gaming exercises, participatory foresight processes and so on, have been developed for various reasons: to support better decision making, better innovation and better interaction between science and society. Yet, it has remained unclear how the effects of such tools should be measured: do they really achieve the aims they promise to achieve?

This book came to be written as a partial answer to this question, one which it is more and more pertinent to address, as the number of vendors offering new tools and remedies for public participation has recently increased. The book does this by summarising the key results of an EU funded research project 'Public Engagement Innovations for Horizon 2020' (PE2020). Encouraged by the prominent members of the scientific advisory board of this project, Suzanne de Cheveigné, Martin Hynes, Edward Andersson, and Markku Mattila, the authors of this study decided to offer the manuscript to Routledge, who considered that it fitted its Focus series as a contribution to topical debates about science in society in Europe and globally. The aim of this book is to give insights of the current developments of public participation and where the development is leading. In this volume we will mainly focus on the contribution of public participation toward better governance of research and innovation, in particular, how it can help in the planning of research programmes and definition of research projects, by providing, for example, knowledge on societally relevant research topics, new participatory approaches and access to financial and cultural resources.

The empirical basis of this book is based on the 'stories' of 38 innovative public participation processes that were collected from Europe and the U.S. during 2014. We are grateful to the following managers of these projects, who provided us with systematic accounts of the processes studied: Luigi Amodio, Edward Andersson, Bjørn Bedsted, Bliss Browne, Jozefien De Marrée, Benoît Derenne, Kathryn de Ridder-Vignone, Niina Ekstam,

David Farrell, Katri Grenman, Julia Hahn, Hans Colind Hansen, Anders Hoff, Maja Horst, Meelika Hirmo, Rachel Iredale, Anke Jesse, Lars Klüver, Rudolf Lewanski, Emma Longridge, Carolyn Lukensmeyer, Katja Machill, Phil Macnaghten, Katja Maaß, Marzia Mazzonetto, Francesco Molinari, Henk Mulder, Richard Pieper, Elizabeth Pollitzer, Jane Randall, Min Reuchamps, Jan Riise, Maria Ritola, Raymond Seltz, Maija Sirola, Frans Snik, Seirian Sumner, Lotta Tomasson, Jaquet Vincent, Diana Wernisch, and Erika Widegren.

We gratefully acknowledge the funding provided by the European Commission to the PE2020 project, the aim of which was to identify, analyse and refine innovative public engagement tools and instruments for dynamic governance in the field of Science in Society. PE2020 analysed such tools and instruments through a systemic and contextual perspective, and paid particular attention to the potential and transferability of new governance innovations based on participation. The main contributions of this project included a *conceptual model of public participation* (introduced in this book) that puts it in a systemic perspective as a tool for dynamic and responsible governance of research; a *catalogue of PE innovations* in Europe and beyond that was used as an important empirical source of this study; *piloting best practice public participation processes* related to the societal challenges of Horizon 2020; and an easily accessible web-based PE design toolkit that helps researchers, researchers managers and planers to design public participation practices in their respective organisations. For any reader interested in these and other resources related to these themes, we recommend the website of the PE2020 project (www.pe2020.eu/) where these materials are freely available.

This book contains materials and ideas resulting from the PE2020 project that have been refined and further elaborated for this volume. Our warmest thanks go to Ms. Liisa Kallio from the University of Helsinki, who provided invaluable help in transforming the manuscript, originally in the form of a skeleton-like research report to a readable book. Without her questions, comments, editorial support and seeking of additional information, this book never would have materialised.

On behalf of the co-authors,

Mikko Rask
Helsinki, Finland
October 2017

Acknowledgement

This project received funding from the European Union's Seventh Framework Programme for research, technological development and demonstration under grant agreement no. 611826. The sole responsibility for the content of this publication lies with the authors. It does not necessarily reflect the opinion of the European Union. The European Commission is not responsible for any use that may be made of the information contained therein.

Acronyms and abbreviations

ACT	public activism (in Appendix 1 online)
BSE	bovine spongiform encephalopathy, commonly known as mad cow disease
COM	public communication (in Appendix 1 online)
CONS	public consultation (in Appendix 1 online)
COP15	15th meeting of the Conference of Parties to the United Nations Framework Convention on Climate Change
CSO	civil society organisation
DEL	public deliberation (in Appendix 1 online)
EC	European Commission
EU	European Union
GM	genetic modification
ICT	information and communication technologies
MMR	MMR vaccine is an immunisation vaccine against measles, mumps, and rubella
NGO	non-governmental organisation
PAR	public participation (in Appendix 1 online)
PE	public engagement
R&I	research and innovation
RRI	responsible research and innovation
SiS	science in society
S&T	science and technology
UNEP	United Nations Environment Programme

Part I

Analytical framework

How to study public engagement

1 Introduction

PE in the context of research and innovation

Demands on science are increasing constantly.[1] Global social challenges call for fast solutions based on a science capable of integrating different disciplines and research communities, and to dialogue with government, industry and civil society. Science is required to be more transparent and accountable, more communicative and inclusive, more ethically oriented and socially committed. At the same time, the authority and unity of science are becoming weaker, and people's trust in science is decreasing, while paradoxically their expectations about the capacity of science to have large social and economic impacts are increasing.

A 'superman model' of science is emerging. Science is asked to do more, faster and better, often with fewer resources, less time and less institutional support. This is leading to higher levels of competition between research institutions and researchers in order to publish, access funds, attract talent and raise reputation. All these challenges are altering research institutions in their culture, procedures, decision processes and organisational structures. In many cases, these changes are not planned or oriented through policies and measures, but are simply borne by researchers and managers. Many factors make it difficult for research institutions to manage such developments, including internal resistance to change, lack of awareness about the benefits and costs involved, overwhelming demands for responsiveness to societal needs, insufficient skills and knowledge about effective societal engagement, paucity of funding and resources, or absence of a national policy environment supporting change (e.g. Maassen, 2017; Shoemaker, 2011; Regenberg, 2010; Hessels et al., 2009).

The question is therefore whether these changes will finally result in a *drift*, a largely ungoverned and uncoordinated set of processes, or in a *transition*, a shift from one state to another, managed and driven, as far as possible, through specific measures, institutional strategies, science policies and cultural inputs.

Public participation is loaded with high expectations in this context. Beyond specific definitions, it can be understood as being a general approach aimed at getting different actors, cultures, interests and knowledge to inter-act to identify and attain common objectives in terms of governance of research institutions and development of the research process. Public par-ticipation is not the unique possible approach, nor can it be applied alone, but it is one of the more relevant and consolidated approaches. Particularly in the context of the European Union (EU), public participation has been established as one of six main pillars of an emerging policy framework for the EU's research activities – the *Responsible Research and Innovation (RRI)* approach – which, combining various objectives and aspects of the so-called science-society relations, including open access, gender, ethics, science education and governance, is trying to increase the alignment of science with the values, needs and expectations of society. *Public engage-ment (PE)* is mostly used interchangeably with public participation, a term that is perhaps more globally known. However, since 'public engagement' is the term adopted by the European Commission (n.d.a), several European research institutions, as well as the research team behind the project under-lying this study, we have also adopted it as the core concept of this volume.

In the last three decades, PE has developed intensively, stimulated by the actions of some national governments and European institutions, mainly under the pressure of an increasingly wide movement – involving researchers, NGOs, and many other stakeholders – engaged to promote more advanced and democratic forms of governance of science and technology. Many facts provide evidence of this trend, including the increasing number of PE expe-riences in Europe and in other regions of the world; the wide diversifica-tion and specialisation of PE tools (for example, 76 different PE mechanisms applied in 256 PE processes were identified by Mejlgaard and Ravn, 2015); the shaping and consolidation of an increasingly wide community of prac-titioners and experts on PE approaches and techniques; and the increasing interests of researchers on PE, as shown by the growing number of papers, articles and scientific meetings devoted to it. Even though it is well-known that the field of PE is developing fast, it is less clear where the development is leading. Where is the cutting edge of this development? In order to address these issues, *an analysis of the trends and characteristics of innovative PE* is one of the three main tasks of this volume.

Despite active development of PE, its diffusion and impact on science has remained limited, for many reasons. The reform of formal institutions of research are out of phase with rapidly changing science in society. Often PE is merely used as a sophisticated form of science communication, not as a permanent component of science governance. Its diffusion is also limited, since – apart from a few countries – in the great majority of European member states, PE is only occasionally applied by research organisations, and national strategies in this field are still weak or missing altogether. PE practices are often not organically connected to the research organisation's policy cycle and research processes. The risk involved with these tendencies is that they can feed disappointment and dissatisfaction with PE, at least as a potential governance tool. In order to address the potential mismatch between high expectations and reality, and support a healthy development in this field, this volume has set the *study of the different performative functions of innovative PE* as the second of its three main tasks. In particular, we will show how innovative PE processes have contributed to a more dynamic and responsible governance of research and innovation. These concepts (to be fully defined later) refer to the ability of policy making to handle issues effectively in a rapidly changing environment requiring continuous adjustment and dynamic interaction between multiple stakeholders, including society at large.

The third main task of this volume is to *develop a synthetic model for evaluating the impacts and benefits of PE.* As PE activity is becoming commonplace, and public money is increasingly being spent on it, it is critical to evaluate the appropriateness, efficiency and impacts of such investments. We will argue that an up-to-date PE evaluation framework should acknowledge not only the classic evaluation criteria just mentioned, but also take into account the multiple functions of PE, and in particular, its potential roles as a tool for dynamic and responsible governance of research and innovation. In other words, PE can result in new governance capacities, and it can induce important systemic functions that should be acknowledged in any serious evaluation of PE activities. A reader interested in relevant evaluation approaches and criteria should find the synthetic PE evaluation model particularly informative, since many of the existing models have been partial at best.

1.1 Evolution of science in society

Public engagement with science has been enjoying unprecedented development in recent decades. It has become a recurrent issue in the public debate on research and innovation. In some national contexts, specific policies aimed at stimulating PE initiatives have been devised. Over time, a wide scientific literature has developed, addressing PE from a range of perspectives.

To grasp the actual and potential role of PE today, it is necessary to widen the interpretive framework to encompass some broader sociological perspectives: How has the relationship between science and society changed in recent decades? How has the governance of science in society changed respectively? What types of PE paradigm can be discerned?

From a sociological perspective, the changes affecting science are part of a wider array of transformations touching contemporary societies as a whole.

Usually such transformations are represented as a shift from modern society to a new society, to which many names have been given, including, for example, 'post-industrial society' (Bell, 1974), 'information society', 'knowledge society', 'risk society' (Beck, 1992), 'reflexive modernity' (Giddens, 1991), 'liquid society' (Baumann, 2000), 'network society' (Castells, 2000), 'post-modern society' (e.g. Lyotard, 1984), and 'high-speed society' (Rosa, 2013). Most of these models concern the changing relationship between social structures and individual actors. In the context of modern society, social structures (e.g. social norms, behavioural models, social roles and values) and the institutions of modernity supporting and reproducing them (e.g. political institutions, religious institutions, economic institutions, trade unions and public administrations) were strong enough to exert a certain control over individuals and groups (in terms of behaviours, expectations, cultural orientations, worldviews and so forth). Now – under the pressure of a range of factors – such structures and institutions are weakening while the autonomy of individuals (e.g. to make their own choice, to shape their own identity, to develop their own worldview) and the groups they are part of is increasing. These complex dynamics are resulting in accelerated transformations of the society, the impacts of which to science-society relations are difficult to anticipate (see, e.g. Bijker and d'Andrea, 2009).

Various theoretical models have been developed to capture the many changes affecting scientific production. These include, among others, the 'Model1/Mode2' (Gibbons et al., 1994; Nowotny et al., 2003), 'Post-Academic Science' (Ziman, 1996), 'Post-Normal Science' (Funtowicz and Ravetz, 2003), 'Triple Helix' (Leydesdorff and Etzkowitz, 1998), 'Quadruple Helix' (Carayannis and Campbell, 2009) and 'Scientific Agency' (Miah, 2017) models that allow shedding light on some of the main trends of change affecting science as a social institution. To provide an overview, ten common trends emerging from these models are summarised below.

Diffusion of cooperative practices in scientific production

Research is increasingly a collective enterprise made up of programmes involving the coordination of an increasing number of scientists and research institutions. This is also due to the fact that in some areas of research costly and sophisticated equipment are increasingly required, which cannot be provided by single research institutions, and where their use is more efficient and economic, when shared among institutions. Moreover, interaction among research institutions is practically unconstrained, for example thanks to ICTs. Knowledge production is therefore lesser and lesser made within hierarchically organised academic institutions but more and more through horizontal research networks.

Contextualisation

Research is increasingly 'context-driven', in other words, carried out in a context of application, arising from the very work of problem solving and not only governed by the paradigms of traditional disciplines. Consequently, research tends to be 'problem-focused': it is no longer initiated only by the interest of the scientist, but it is aimed at coping with specific problems or seizing a given opportunity.

Socially diffused research

There is a much greater diversity of the sites at which knowledge is produced as well as of the types of knowledge produced. The university is no longer the unique environment for research production.

Transdisciplinarity

Research is increasingly transdisciplinary in nature, while in the past it was carried out narrowly in specific disciplinary domains. Another aspect of the same process is that relationships between universities, governments and industries are increasingly closer and coordinated. This results in the creation of 'hybrid' structures and institutions, such as academic spin-offs, high-tech incubators, and science and technology parks.

Quality control enlargement

Quality control systems are changing, involving actors other than peers (for example, knowledge brokers, final users, citizens) and applying multiple assessment criteria.

Accountability

There is an increasing need to make science accountable to a wide range of actors, with effects such as the proliferation of evaluation exercises and modification of research procedures (for example, disaggregation of transdisciplinary research in order to allow disciplinary-based evaluation).

Utilitarianism

Research results are often expected to have economic impacts. This does not only mean favouring applied research but adopting the potential economic impact as a parameter for assessing any kind of research programme.

Consequently, a discovery is often assessed for its commercial value, even before for its scientific value.

Scientists as experts

In some cases, scientists are asked to support political processes, especially in sectors where facts are uncertain, values are in dispute, stakes are high and decisions urgent. This evidently involves scientists as experts with political decision-making processes, often supporting different and possibly conflicting interpretations, views and positions. This weakens the image of science as a consistent and unitary set of certified knowledge.

Political steering

Policy makers show an increasing desire to lead the research process and to steer research priorities, at both European (through the framework programs) and national levels. This has also led to increasingly competitive access to public research funds.

Bureaucratisation

Research is growingly deferred to bureaucratic and administrative regulations and standardised procedures, related to work security, application for funds, evaluation and assessment, fraud control, and management, for example.

These and other changes affecting scientific production are largely modifying science-society relationships. For a long time, such relationships were limited and institutionally well-regulated, as described by the ivory tower model (Bok, 1984). Now science-society relationships are more intense and complex, invoking new challenges for research governance. For example, decreasing authoritativeness and diminishing social recognition of scientific institutions is driving societies toward anti-science attitudes and pseudo-scientific beliefs. An ever-stronger connection between science and ethical and policy issues is triggering and feeding social tensions on controversial issues and 'public battles' among experts (e.g. Cook, 2014; Caputo, 2010; Rowe et al., 2005). People's decreasing trust in scientific institutions is leading to a growing demand for accountability and transparency (Boaventura de Sousa, 2010). Increasing costs of scientific investments are requesting that science institutions can increasingly demonstrate their social and economic usefulness to citizens as taxpayers.

These factors are plunging science into a paradoxical situation: it has become increasingly important for our life and our future, but at the same time, science has become increasingly fragile as a social institution. It is not by chance that some scholars are speaking about the need for a new social contract allowing science and society to regulate anew their interactions and mutual responsibilities (e.g. Pardo and Calvo, 2002; Gibbons, 1999).

1.2 Changing paradigms of PE

Box 1.1   General definition of public engagement (PE)

PE refers to a range of participatory processes, through which there is a *distinct* role for citizens and stakeholder groups to contribute to research and innovation activities.

In this volume, we have adopted a quite general definition of PE (Box 1.1). This is to ensure an open exploration of the different modalities of PE activity, ranging from science communication to public deliberation and public activism; from bottom-up to top-down processes of interaction. In fact, PE is also one of the many concepts which is susceptible to different and even contrasting interpretations and uses, ranging from those that are restricted in scope and technical in nature, up to those that are large in scope and almost philosophical in nature. Some alternative definitions of public engagement in science and society are provided in Box 1.2.

Box 1.2   Alternative definitions of PE

National Co-ordinating Centre for Public Engagement (2017):

Public engagement describes the myriad ways in which the activity and benefits of higher education and research can be shared with the public. Engagement is by definition a two-way process, involving interaction and listening, with the goal of generating mutual benefit.

AAAS Center for Public Engagement with Science and Technology (n.a.):

Public engagement with science describes intentional, meaningful interactions that provide opportunities for mutual learning between scientists and members of the public. Mutual learning refers not just to the acquisition of knowledge, but also to increased familiarity with a breadth of perspectives, frames, and worldviews. Goals for public engagement with science in addition to mutual learning, include civic engagement skills and empowerment, increased awareness of the cultural relevance of science, and recognition of the importance of multiple perspectives and domains of knowledge to scientific endeavours.

High Education Funding Council of England (2007):

'Public engagement' involves specialists in higher education listening to, developing their understanding of, and interacting with non-specialists. The 'public' includes individuals and groups who do not currently have a formal relationship with a higher education institution through teaching, research or knowledge transfer.

Association of Commonwealth Universities (2001):

Engagement implies strenuous, thoughtful, argumentative interaction with the non-university world in at least four spheres: setting universities' aims, purposes, and priorities; relating teaching and learning to the wider world; the back-and-forth dialogue between researchers and practitioners; and taking on wider responsibilities as neighbours and citizens.

Committee on Institutional Cooperation (2005):

Engagement is the partnership of university knowledge and resources with those of the public and private sectors to enrich scholarship, research, and creative activity; enhance curriculum, teaching and learning; prepare educated, engaged citizens; strengthen democratic values and civic responsibility; address critical societal issues; and contribute to the public good. . . . The publicly engaged institution is fully committed to direct, two-way interaction with communities and other external constituencies through the development, exchange, and application of knowledge, information, and expertise for mutual benefit.

Despite the many alternative definitions of PE, there is a general consensus at least since the beginning of this century, that a shift from communication-oriented PE to dialogue-oriented PE has occurred. After several years punctuated by scientific and technological controversies – over BSE, genetically modified crops, applications of nanotechnology, mobile phones, nuclear waste, the MMR vaccine, and so forth – more and more scientists and engineers have recognised the need to become more open and accountable. Consequently, there are increasing interests in hearing and heeding public voices early enough, at a time when they can still influence research priorities. As the European Commission (2008) report on science in society has suggested following Wilsdon and Willis (2004), the evolution of PE in Europe can be discerned under three different phases or 'paradigms' of PE activity, including 'public understanding of science', 'public dialogue' and 'upstream engagement' (Box 1.3). Naturally, any history of complex processes such as PE is in reality more multilinear due to various local and national idiosyncrasies. However, as the three-phase model identified by the European Commission (2008) report suggests, there have also been some common trends in PE development, driven mainly by some Europe-wide crises of science that have influenced the research and innovation policy thinking both at the national and transnational levels.

Box 1.3   Three phases of public engagement

Phase 1: Public understanding of science

The initial response of scientists to growing levels of public detachment and mistrust was to embark on a mission to inform. Attempts to gauge levels of public understanding date back to the early 1970s, and have regularly uncovered gaps in people's knowledge of scientific facts. In the UK, Sir Walter Bodmer's influential 1985 report for the Royal Society argued that 'It is clearly a part of each scientist's professional responsibility to promote the public understanding of science'.

Phase 2: From deficit to dialogue

However, implicit in the language and methods of 'public understanding of science' was a flawed understanding of science, a flawed understanding of the public, and a flawed understanding of understanding. It relied on a 'deficit' model of the public, which assumed that if only people were told more about science, they would fall in line behind it. In 2000, an influential UK House of Lords report detected 'a new mood for dialogue'. In 2002, at the EU level, the first Science and Society programme was incorporated in the sixth Research Framework Programme with new initiatives around public participation. The language of 'science and society' became prominent, and there was a fresh impetus towards accountability and engagement. In the five years since, there was a perceptible change. The science community adopted a more conversational tone in its dealings with the public, if not always with enthusiasm, then at least out of a recognition that new forms of engagement are now a non-negotiable clause of their licence to operate.

Phase 3: Upstream engagement

Yet despite this progress, the links from public engagement back to the choices, priorities and everyday practices of science remained fuzzy and unclear. Dialogue tended to be restricted to particular questions, posed at particular stages in the cycle of research, development and exploitation. Possible risks were endlessly debated, while deeper questions about the values, visions, and vested interests that motivate scientific endeavour often remained unasked or unanswered. And as the genetic modification (GM) case vividly demonstrates, when these larger issues force themselves onto the table, the public may discover that it is too late to alter the trajectories of a technology. Political, economic and organisational commitments may already be in place, narrowing the space for meaningful debate. More recently, there has been a wave of interest in moving public engagement 'upstream' – to an earlier stage in the processes of research and development. There is a sense that earlier controversies have created a window of opportunity, through which we can see more clearly how to reform and improve the governance of science and technology. Most immediately, policymakers and the science community are desperate to avoid developments in fields like nanotechnology, neuroscience and synthetic biology becoming 'the next GM'. The wounds of that battle are still raw, and there is little appetite for a rerun.

(European Commission, 2008, pp. 16–17)

While the European Commission report (2008) refers to the different phases in the history of PE until the end of the 2000s, some more recent studies have detected the trends and patterns of PE since the early 2010s. One of them is the MASIS (Monitoring Policy and Research Activities on Science in Society in Europe) project (2010–2012) that surveyed science-in-society practices across 37 European countries. The analysis identified heterogeneous models and levels of PE in science and technology decision making in Europe (Mejlgaard et al., 2012). It found out that while many countries have introduced formalised procedures for involving citizens in priority-setting and assessment of research and innovation, the actual degree of public involvement differs significantly among European countries. Generally modest and highly unequal performance levels among European countries studied were also found by Rask, Mačiukaitė-Žvinienė et al. (2012), who constructed a model of 'participatory performance' that they used to analyse the MASIS data basis. The levels of participatory performance were measured by identifying the number of structures and processes supporting open dialogues and public deliberation on research and innovation per country (Figure 1.1). The higher the 'participatory performance', in Figure 1.1, the more there was evidence of the country supporting public dialogues on SiS issues and possessing structures to host deliberations contributing to STI governance (see Rask, Mačiukaitė-Žvinienė et al., 2012; cf. Dryzek, 2009). Furthermore, in that paper, the different performance levels were explained through a Porterian approach, including 'participatory resources', 'demand conditions', 'related and supportive factors', and 'governmental strategies and approaches' as explanatory factors (see, Porter, 1998; Rask et al., 2012).

As Figure 1.1 suggests, participatory performance is highest in Western European countries. Two countries with highest levels of performance measured are the UK and Switzerland – obviously two countries with very different political systems, one with a long history of constitutional monarchy and parliamentary politics, the other with a federal parliamentary democracy with strong elements of direct democracy. All grade B countries are located in the east of Europe. We can therefore assume that the past division of Eastern and Western Europe still plays a role in explaining the differences in cultures of public participation, while there are obviously many other explanatory factors.

In the following section we comment on how this volume will contribute to the discussion on PE, by focusing on the following three research topics: 'trend tracking' of new PE activities (*innovativeness*); developing of new conceptualisations about the *functions of PE*, especially as a tool for governing research; and proposing better ways for the *evaluation of PE*.

1.3 Current issues in PE research

Current development trends and functions of PE have been approached in several studies, like the question of how to evaluate such processes. These questions were studied, both empirically and theoretically, in the PE2020 project on the results of which this volume builds. In the following subsections, we will indicate the unique contributions of this volume on these research streams.

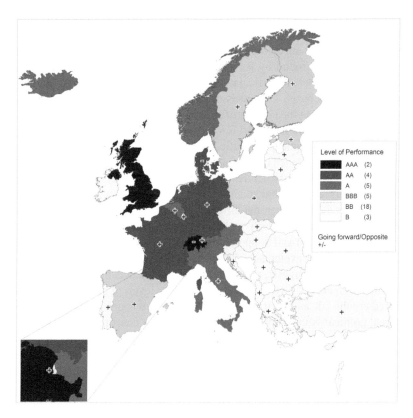

Figure 1.1 Participatory performance of nations

Source: Rask, Mačiukaitė-Žvinienė et al. (2012). The countries are ranked in six categories, best performing countries indicated with maximum (AAA) rates and worst performing countries with minimum (B) rates. Countries where participatory development is reported to go forward are indicated by a plus (+) sign and where the opposite is true by minus (−) sign.

Innovativeness

Innovations in PE have attracted considerable attention by scholars from a range of fields. Scholars of democracy have studied innovations in democracy and democratic deliberation (e.g. Grönlund et al., 2014; Smith, 2009), while researchers in innovation studies have tracked new ways of involving users, consumers and 'prosumers' in the development of new products and services (e.g. Hyysalo et al., 2016; Ritzer et al., 2012). Overall, there appear to be two completely different places for involving 'the public': first, in identifying the 'public interest' and orientating the boundary conditions for science and technology, and secondly, involving real actors, mostly users, in shaping real technology (products, systems). As the MASIS expert group on science in society issues states:

> the notion of 'participation' has a double meaning. While initially it was an issue in theories of democracy, claiming a renewal of the more formal representative democracy and enriching it by forms of a deliberative and interactive democracy, it is now also used to describe the involvement of users in the shaping of specific technologies which would be sensible in many cases but does not have much to do with political democracy. Public participation loses its traditional and emphatic connotation of deliberative democracy and becomes more and more a means of involving users in the design of new products, driven by economic rather than political needs.
>
> (European Commission, 2009)

Unique in the PE2020 data base is that it covers examples of both public interest and product oriented PE processes, and actually, it expands the scope of analysis to 'public activism', which is a category rarely included in studies of 'orchestrated' PE processes. The data basis is also unique in providing probably the broadest sample of innovative PE processes in the field of R&I thus far collected: the sample was built on the basis of the MASIS (2010–2012) data base, which covered SiS activities in 37 European countries; the data were completed by circulating a new survey within the EU funded PE2020 project (2014–2017) and merging it with yet another set of data collected by an EU-funded sister project, Engage2020 (2013–2015). Resulting from the broad scope of this data base (fully described in Chapter 2), we suggested a new way of classifying the PE methods, and produced new knowledge on the innovative aspects of cutting-edge PE (Chapter 6).

Contrary to some earlier studies on PE, which paid attention to the limited impacts of PE and criticised PE from the tendency of remaining an 'intramural' exercise (e.g. Grönlund et al., 2014; Kies and Nanz, 2013; Rask, 2013; Goodin and Dryzek, 2006; Rip, 2003), *we found innovative PE to have truly diverse impacts*, not only on R&I but also on environment, society, politics – and individuals. We distinguished between three impact areas – substantive, practical and normative – and we found that close to *three-quarters of the reported impacts could be described as practical*. This is an interesting finding, since there is much talk about the rationales of PE: should it be driven by democratic, epistemic or pragmatic motivations? Our empirical finding is that innovative PE largely contributes to practical issues, such as cognitive and attitudinal changes (e.g. better awareness of environmental and scientific issues), development of new capacities (e.g. new professional skills, methods and platforms of collaboration), and mobilisation of resources for addressing scientific and societal challenges (e.g. research funding, political commitment, public awareness, and social acceptance). A subcategory of practical impacts includes impacts on policy making (e.g. development of policy recommendations, informing R&I policy making with citizens' viewpoints, and joint definition of research agendas).

Another type of impact identified was normative impact, such as democratisation and increasing responsibility of research, which are at the core of the RRI approach (see Section 3.2). Instances of normative impacts included consensus building, community building, political empowerment, increased gender equality in science, and introduction of the principles of deliberative democracy to R&I governance. *We observed that innovative PE only limitedly had a substantive impact, in other words, contributed to new scientific knowledge.* Considering that our primary focus has been on PE projects related to R&I, this can be seen as a disappointing result. However, there were important deviations to this pattern. Citizen science and science shops (organisations within universities or other knowledge institutes that conduct scientific research on behalf of citizens and local civil society, see Beunen et al., 2012), in particular, emerged as new concepts that not only involve co-design, but also co-implementation of R&I.

Functions of PE

Functions of PE have been studied from many different angles. A classic example is the 'Spectrum of public participation' by the International Association for Public Participation (IAP2, 2007). It distinguishes between five main functions of PE: information, consultation, involvement, collaboration and empowerment. The IAP2 model also acknowledges different promises of PE to the public. For example, the promise of information, simply, is to keep the public informed, while the promise of involvement is to ensure that public concerns are reflected in the alternatives developed by decision makers, and that the public will be provided with feedback on how its input influenced the decision. Another relevant example is the 'risk management escalator' model of stakeholder involvement (Renn, 2008). The model aims to allocate different risks to be treated through different discourses and actors involved. Yet another example is an EU-funded project TEPSIE (the Theoretical, Empirical and Policy Foundations for Building Social Innovation in Europe), which constructed a typology based on two basic functions of PE (either in providing information about the present state or developing future solutions) and small versus large-scale involvement strategies applied.

These and other similar models that distinguish between the functions of PE tend to be oriented towards specific purposes (for example, defining risk management strategies) and they are often normative in nature (informing about relevant management strategies). The model of 'participatory performance' elaborated in the PE2020 project involves a new specific feature of such models: *it focuses on the identification of the new capacities that PE can contribute to dynamic and responsible governance of R&I*. While the frame of this model is therefore highly theoretical, its orientation, unlike in the models mentioned previously, is fully descriptive: it is oriented at empirically analysing the ways in which such capacities become produced through PE practices.

In summary, the 'composite model of participatory performance' developed in this study explains how different functions and capacities of PE contribute to dynamic and responsible governance of R&I. We found that 'public reflection on R&I' is by far the most general function of innovative PE, followed by the capacities of anticipation and strengthening of transdisciplinary research. Quite interestingly, we found also that creation of continuity is becoming a more important capacity that is needed both to balance dynamic governance, and to sustain dynamism in the long run. Continuity was created through different types of institutional boundary work, for example, multi-level policy communication (local-national-international), multi-actor collaboration (public-private-people) and different types of political embedding. These and other findings regarding participatory performance are discussed in Chapter 7.

Evaluation of PE

Evaluation of PE has stimulated considerable attention in recent years, by scholars and practitioners of PE. In Chapter 8 we identify the various types of evaluation literature, including meta-evaluations, academic evaluation studies, handbooks, theoretical discussion on evaluation frameworks, and evaluations intended for practitioners.

A classic distinction between different evaluation frameworks is between formative and summative evaluations. Formative evaluations are conducted during programme development and implementation and are useful in the direction of how best to achieve project goals or improve project performance. Summative evaluations, respectively, should be completed once a project is well-established or completed, and the purpose is to clarify whether the project has achieved its goals. Some interesting recently developed evaluation approaches include 'realist evaluation' that is an emerging methodology, which explicitly addresses complexity in social interventions and processes, relevant for public engagement. It integrates qualitative and quantitative methods, emphasises 'learning' and applies multiple methods such as quantitative, qualitative, comparative and narrative evidence, as well as 'grey literature' (materials and research produced by organisations outside of the traditional academic publishing and distribution channels) and the insights of programme staff. The idea is to use the data and evidence gathered to 'test' the theory or theories of change under consideration and how well they explain the pattern of outcomes (Wellcome Trust, 2015). Some other recent models include 'Outcome Mapping', a participatory monitoring and evaluation approach that sees projects' outcomes as changes in the behaviour and activities of partners that the project directly influences, and the 'Most Significant Change' approach that is a qualitative and participatory monitoring and evaluation approach that uses stories of change to assess the impact of projects and programmes (Wellcome Trust, 2015).

In this volume, we are not proposing a new evaluation approach. Rather, we are contributing to the discussion on relevant evaluation perspectives, by proposing a structured set of evaluation criteria, based on some theoretical models and empirical findings. As explained earlier, we propose a 'synthetic model of PE evaluation' that acknowledges not only the classic evaluation criteria (appropriateness, efficiency and impacts), but more importantly, targets the evaluation to the different functions and capacities of PE as a tool for dynamic and responsible governance of research and innovation. An underlying idea is to broaden the evaluation from the habitual 'event focused' approach toward a more systemic approach, also acknowledging broader systemic and institutional impacts as well as indirect impacts, such as creation of spin-offs, so often reported from real life example of PE. Actually, the main strength of the synthetic model of PE evaluation is that it is based on a broad sample of empirical PE cases: the test case for each of the criteria proposed is that they have been identified as important by more than one manager of recently conducted PE projects. The idea of the synthetic model of PE evaluation is not to provide a ready-made universal evaluation framework but rather, to provide a solid and broad enough starting point for any evaluation process that is interested in capturing the most essential features and impacts of PE, based on up-to-date research.

Note

1 The introductory chapter relies on d'Andrea and Caiati (2016), in which more information and references to research literature can be found. The remaining chapters are based on Rask et al. (2016). Both of these publications are results of the PE2020 project.

2 Methodology
Exploring and evaluating innovative PE processes

An unspoken rule of any methodology is that it has to fit the nature of the problem at hand. The original idea of the PE2020, the project underlying this volume, was to explore the different functions of PE in the context of research and innovation activities. Starting from the concept of 'participatory performance' (Rask, Mačiukaitė-Žvinienė et al., 2012), and shifting the focus from national debates on R&I to the PE activities in the context of research projects and programmes, some new questions emerged, including the following: Do PE processes in the latter contexts imply functions other than debating and deliberating? What specific benefits and challenges are related to PE in these contexts? What innovative PE practices are currently being introduced in Europe and globally? How could we characterise innovativeness and the success of PE at the level of research programmes and projects?

In order to study these questions, the main methodology adopted was one of *explorative case studies*. An international sample of innovative PE cases was built, and a methodology for exploring the cases was designed. The data and methods of this exploration will be described in the following sections.

2.1 Data collection on PE innovations

The data used in this study consist of an *inventory* of European and U.S. PE innovations, realised between 1992 and 2016, encompassing 256 initiatives and 76 PE 'mechanisms' (Ravn et al., 2014), and a *catalogue* of 38 innovative PE cases (Mejlgaard and Ravn, 2015) representing cutting-edge PE practices, analysed in depth and across different engagement categories and objectives. These data are described in the following subsections.

Inventory of PE mechanisms and initiatives

The analysis of current developments of PE was initiated with the collection of data on PE innovations, the so-called inventory. The first task of the data collection was twofold: to construct a systematically ordered inventory of PE innovations in Europe and beyond, and to crystallise an analytical approach that is able to capture variation in their objectives and formats. As an empirical starting point, 37 national country reports of a previous European project were examined: Monitoring Policy and Research Activities on Science in Society in Europe (MASIS, 2010–12), but a significant and a more up-to-date input was reached through co-operation with the simultaneously organised Engaging Society in Horizon 2020 project (Engage2020). The Engage2020 project conducted a survey among international scholars in the field of R&I, in order to map the use of PE methods in activities related to R&I. The PE2020 inventory added in these survey results when supplementary mechanisms and specific initiatives were identified. Furthermore, a literature review was conducted comprising both academic journals and non-academic reports addressing PE activities. The academic journals *Public Understanding of Science, Science, Technology, and Human Values, Science Communication*, and *Science and Public Policy* were examined for recent articles concerning 'public engagement', since these journals represent primary outlets for academic analysis of PE activities. This systematic procedure included recent articles published between 2008 and 2015. External sources such as the internet (for example, homepages of institutions, organisations and centres engaged with PE activities) supplemented the data collection. Additional cases suggested by project partners and international advisory board members were also added to the inventory.

The main categories of PE tools in the inventory are presented under the five headings specified in Box 2.1: public communication, public consultation, public deliberation, public participation and public activism. Compared to Mejlgaard and Ravn (2015), however, we have adopted a broader understanding of 'public activism', including not only flow of information to decision makers, but also direct implementation of change, as for example in the case of Let's do it!, where toxic wastes were cleaned from the environment. In addition, a simple, dual classification scheme distinguishing between PE mechanisms (which are generic ways of enacting PE) and PE initiatives (which are concrete examples of specific engagement activities) was applied to the inventory. This classification functions as a means to arrange the cases in an accessible and informative way, and its aim is to reduce complexity in a highly complex database.

Box 2.1   Categories of PE

Public communication – the aim is to inform and/or educate citizens. The flow of information constitutes one-way communication from sponsors to public representatives, and no specific mechanisms exist to handle public feedback (examples include public hearings, public meetings and awareness raising activities).

Public consultation – the aim is to inform decision-makers of public opinions on certain topics. These opinions are sought from the sponsors of the PE initiative and no prescribed dialogue is implemented. Thus, in this case, the one-way communication is conveyed from citizens to sponsors (examples include citizens' panels, planning cells and focus groups).

Public deliberation – the aim is to facilitate group deliberation on policy issues of where the outcome may impact decision-making. Information is exchanged between sponsors and public representatives and a certain degree of dialogue is facilitated. The flow of information constitutes two-way communication (examples include 'mini publics' such as consensus conferences, citizen juries and deliberative opinion polling).

Public participation – the aim is to assign partly or fully decision-making-power on policy issues to citizens. Information is exchanged between sponsors and public representatives and a certain degree of dialogue is facilitated. The flow of information constitutes two-way communication (examples include co-governance and direct democracy mechanisms such as participatory budgeting, youth councils and binding referendums).

Public activism – the aim is to inform decision-makers and create awareness in order to influence decision-making processes. The information flow is conveyed in one-way communication from citizens to sponsors but not on the initiative of the sponsors as characterises the 'public consultation' category (examples include demonstrations and protests).

(Source: Mejlgaard and Ravn, 2015)

Catalogue of public engagement innovations

While the inventory provided a good starting point, it was not a sufficient database in terms of depth of information for the analysis of PE developments. The second task of the data collection was therefore to identify a number of PE initiatives for in-depth exploration, in terms of innovative characteristics, orientation towards societal challenges, advantages and obstacles and so forth. As a basis for selecting the case studies included in the catalogue, a nomination procedure was implemented, that included the full consortium and the international advisory board (ten nominators in total). Each nominator was invited to select and rank the most innovative initiatives using a tailored template for this purpose. Nominators were to take into account the preliminary criteria of innovativeness delineated below, and they were requested to qualify each nominated initiative by providing a reflection on the initiative on the backdrop of the selection criteria. If supplementary criteria were used for nomination, each nominator was asked to state those as well.

The following six pre-constructed criteria of innovativeness were applied in the case selection and qualification (Mejlgaard and Ravn, 2015): hybrid combinations; methodological novelty; inclusive new ways of representation; potential impact; bearing on societal challenges; and feasibility. The criteria put forth were based on prior theoretical and empirical knowledge of the field, and in line with the explorative approach, they remained fairly open, inclusive and broad in order to reach a more comprehensive assessment of innovativeness and to deepen and complement our evolving understanding of the notion of innovativeness in PE. On the basis of the nomination process, a total of 62 nominations were obtained. Subsequently, case coordinators were identified as informants of the survey. Based on a common contact protocol, each consortium partner personally contacted a number of case coordinators with information on the project and the objectives of the survey. Upon these personal contacts between the consortium partners and the informants, 56 questionnaires were dispatched. Following a procedure of reminders and follow-up contacts with targeted informants, 38 case descriptions were collected.

The catalogue of PE innovations is a collection of detailed case descriptions and reflections provided by individual case coordinators with particular expertise related to the initiative in question. The approach of including expert descriptions allowed for in-depth and firsthand reflections, experiences and information at a level of detail which would have been difficult to access otherwise. Each coordinator completed an open-ended survey exploring key features of the initiative, including the innovative dimensions of the particular PE case, outcomes and impacts, case relations to policy decision-making processes, and advantages and challenges associated with the case and according to the Horizon 2020 societal challenges. The common survey structure allowed for horizontal comparisons of PE innovations, while the open and qualitative approach simultaneously enabled a more inductive and nuanced examination of the concept and features of innovative practices. Each case was classified according to the following main categories:

- *PE category* – See Box 2.1.
- *Mechanism* – Generic ways of enacting public engagement, for example, consensus conference, participatory budgeting.

- *Main purpose of initiative* – Awareness raising, education and capacity building, protest, community building, consultation, dialogue/deliberation, knowledge co-production, co-governance.
- *Geographical scale* – Global, European, national, regional, local/urban and institutional.
- *Organising entity* – National governmental body, local governmental body, academic institution, NGO, community-based organisation, non-profit organisation, science museum/centre, industry and business.
- *Target groups* – Lay publics, researchers, stakeholder organisations/ groups, experts, public officials.
- *H2020 Societal Challenges* – See Box 6.2.

2.2 Two empirical analysis methods for understanding different perspectives of innovative PE projects and programmes

For the analysis of the data on PE innovations, two complementary methodological approaches were chosen, in order to get a rich understanding of the dimensions of innovative PE. One working group of the PE2020 research consortium carried out a qualitative content analysis (Consumer Society Research Centre at the University of Helsinki, Finland), while another group conducted a quantitative analysis using descriptive statistics (Vilnius University International Business School, Lithuania). The results were compared and used as a means to validate the findings.

Qualitative analysis included content analysis of each public engagement case description. Such an approach was chosen to explore a variety of issues emerging with PE, regarded particularly as a tool for governing research issues. The findings were reported through *cognitive maps* (Appendix 1 online). The content analysis applied both, so to say, bottom-up (referring to the point of view of the promoters of the PE processes) and top-down (referring to the point of the view of the PE2020 project team) approaches. The analysis involved a close reading of the issues emerging with the particular cases in particular contexts. Such issues were coded and aggregated into relevant clusters. To make such analyses comparable, several rounds of analysis, clustering, harmonisation and validation of the codes were carried out. The analysis resulted in a series of cognitive maps, providing a highly unique 'footprint' for each PE case (Figure 2.1).

Figure 2.1 provides the reading instructions for the cognitive maps provided in Appendix 1 online. The left-hand side of the map illustrates the 'input side' of the PE process: resources, structures, strategies and contextual factors that were involved in the design and implementation of the case. The right-hand side of the map illustrates the 'output side'. This includes learning effects,

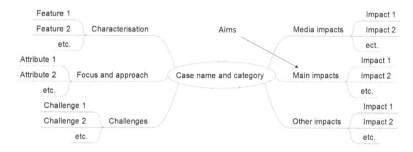

Figure 2.1 A reading instruction for the cognitive maps in Appendix 1 (online)

policy and media impacts, networking and various spin-off effects. As illustrated in Figure 2.1, the cognitive maps include the following components:

- *The title and category* (for the categories, see Box 2.1).
- *A short characterisation* (including a description of their main functions and political contexts).
- *Focus and approach* (including the methodological features, organisational and institutional strategies and other factors related to the design and implementation of the projects).
- *The main aims* (the main aims were not necessarily those that were described in the original plan of the PE process, since in some cases the aims were amended as a response to emerging issues while implementing the case).
- *The main impacts* (the arrow between main impacts and main aims is to draw readers' attention to the congruence or discrepancy between the intended aims and realised effects).
- *Media impacts* (in cases when those were reported).
- *Challenges and obstacles* encountered during the implementation.

Quantitative analysis, on the other hand, is more characterised by a top-down approach, where variables related to innovativeness, impacts and success were derived from research literature (Mačiukaitė-Žvinienė et al., 2014). If the qualitative approach was used to explore emerging issues, the quantitative approach was chosen to complement this picture, by starting from such factors that are known to be relevant, when explaining the characteristics and success of PE processes, for example, the 'owners' and institutional backgrounds of PE processes, as well as the scope and application of different categories of methods applied. The contents of the statistical analyses are described in Table 2.1. The fact sheets can be found in Appendices 2–6 online.

Table 2.1 Contents of the statistical analysis

> **Communication patterns and participant selection - Appendix 2**
>
> - What methods were used for participant selection? *(controlled, uncontrolled, self-selection)*
> - What types of communication were used? *(face-to-face, media, mixed)*
> - What types of media were used? *(printed, translated, internet-based, other)*
> - How many different media were used?
> - What was the level of communication? *(one way, two way)*
> - How was communication directed? *(sponsor to public, public to sponsor, public to public)*
> - What formal evidence was introduced?
> - Was the PE initiative transdisciplinary?

> **PE categories and mechanisms - Appendices 3 and 4**
>
> - What was the main category of PE? *(public communication, activism, consultation, deliberation and participation)*?
> - What were the PE mechanisms? *(out of 76 mechanisms identified in Deliverable 1.1)*

> **Impact areas, learning and continuity - Appendix 5**
>
> - In which area were the aims of PE initiatives fulfilled in (culture, government, society, science and technology)? *(impact areas)*
> - Was the PE initiative repeated? *(continuity)*
> - Were there signs of methodological reflection after the end of PE initiative? *(lessons learnt)*
> - Did the organiser of PE have determination or intention to elaborate the PE concept? *(liability for changes, adaptability)*

> **Features of innovativeness - Appendix 6**
>
> - What are the features of innovativeness of PE per cases? *(hits in a list of 17 innovative characteristics)*

2.3 Limitations and validity of the results

There are two main limitations to the validity of the results related to the data. First, 38 cases is a small sample, especially for a statistical study. The authors of this volume are aware of this limitation, and therefore refrain from drawing too firm conclusions from such analysis. Furthermore, it remains uncertain what we could have learned from the 26 cases for which there was no response to our survey. To compensate, however, the quantitative analysis was only one aspect of this study; the main emphasis was in the qualitative study and exploration of the issues emerging with innovative PE.

The second limitation is related to the quality of the data. The data were provided by the coordinators of recently finished or ongoing PE processes. Since it is in the interest of the project managers to promote their own activities, we expected there to be a positive bias in these reports. However, we found that these reports also included critical reflections on the challenges and obstacles met during different stages of the PE processes, which we consider to reflect the honesty and learning orientation of these reports. Furthermore, and to justify our strategy of data collection, it should be noted that for many recent PE projects, published reports were not available, and that the PE managers' reports therefore include inside knowledge that would not have been available through alternative research approaches. In some cases, when published materials were available, we have consulted them to provide further insights on the cases studied.

The validity of the analysis was strengthened by iterating the analyses, seeking feedback from colleagues, and comparing the qualitative content analysis with the quantitative analysis, and making any necessary adjustments. At the same time, it is worth recognising that some degree of subjectivity is unavoidable in this kind of work.

3   Conceptual framework

PE as part of dynamic and responsible governance of R&I

The conceptual framework of this study includes the logics of analysis, in other words, the 'analytical framework', and a definition of the key concepts used throughout the volume. The purpose of the conceptual framework is to orient the analysis towards the key issues of this study: how PE can contribute to more dynamic and responsible governance of R&I.

3.1 Analytical framework

The analytical framework of this study is described in Figure 3.1. It acknowledges the context of this study, nominates the key 'analytical lenses' used in the focusing of the empirical research, and delineates the main theoretical concepts and discussions.

Starting with some contextual observations, PE is a phenomenon which can be related, and is increasingly linked to different domains of activity. Urban planning and environmental decision making are examples of two domains, where public participation has been among mainstream paradigms for several decades, even though competing with other paradigms of planning and decision making (e.g. Forester, 1989; Dietz and Stern, 2008). In the domain of R&I, instead, the adaptation of PE has been somewhat slower, even though in recent years things have changed towards being more receptive, as discussed in the introductory chapter.

The domain of R&I is large. It ranges from academic basic research and applied research to various co-creation and innovation activities, also including research policy making and the funding of research, as well as a broad category of science-in-society (SiS) activity. *In this volume, we are mainly interested in understanding the role of PE at the level of research projects and programmes.* These are two of the four levels of research and innovation policy activity, distinguished by the PE2020 project, following a similar distinction by our sister project Engage2020. The most general level is policy formation, which includes the design and creation of large R&I

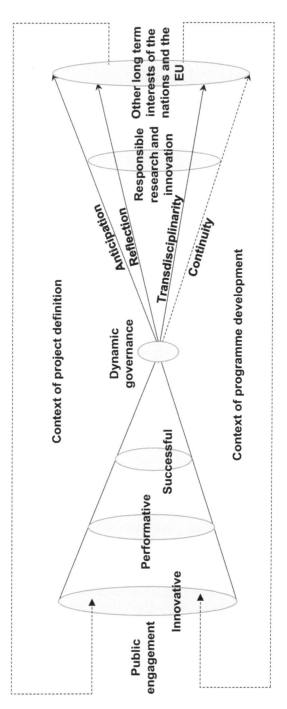

Figure 3.1 Analytical framework

policy issues, including research infrastructures and organisational settings that provide the frame conditions of conducting research and innovation activities. Another level is programme development, which includes funding schemes, thematic prioritisation and other general rules and guidelines for researchers and research funders. The third level is project definition, which refers to the delineation of the research topics, methods applied and resources included in specific research projects. The fourth level includes research and innovation activities, which are the actual activities carried out by research actors in order to accomplish the objectives of R&I projects. PE may or may not be relevant in any of these four levels. Programme development and project definition are places where PE, in principle, can be straightforwardly applied, in steering research to societally relevant goals and designing new interactions between science and society.

Located in this context, Figure 3.1 illustrates the logics of this study. The left-hand side of the funnel refers to the 'analytical lenses' that focus the empirical research. The right-hand side of the figure, on the other hand, refers to the key capacities of dynamic governance, the role of which will be discussed in the context of RRI. The key concepts explaining the logics of analysis will be defined next.

3.2 Definition of the key concepts

There are many ways to define the five key concepts of this study: 'innovativeness', 'participatory performance', 'successfulness', 'dynamic governance' and 'responsible research and innovation'. The operational definitions for each of these concepts will be given in the boxes below, followed by a discussion on how we intend to use them.

Several academic discussions are related to these concepts. *Innovation* has been studied, for several decades, within innovation studies, however, with somewhat limited attention to the particular types of innovation related to PE activities. '*Participatory performance*', instead, is a quite new concept, introduced in Rask, Mačiukaitė-Žvinienė et al. (2012) and elaborated here to help thinking about the different functions and intensities of PE activity in the project and programme contexts. *Successfulness*, in turn, is a basic concept in evaluation studies, as discussed in Chapter 8. *Dynamic governance* is an interesting concept, as there is not actually much academic discussion around it, even though it makes much sense in describing the current 'realities' of policy making, including tendencies toward lean management and increased efficiency requests in public policy making; the EU has also acknowledged it as among the guiding principles of R&I governance (for instance, the PE2020 project responded to a research call inviting new opening toward 'dynamic governance or R&I). Finally, 'responsible research and innovation' is a clear example of a 'policy concept', backed with some academic research that is used to delineate research activities and provide a framework for EU's current research policy. These concepts will be introduced next, and as the latter two are in an interesting but somewhat ambiguous relation, we have offered some commentary about their relationship.

Innovativeness

Box 3.1   Innovative PE

Innovative PE can be defined as new participatory tools and methods that have the potential to contribute to a more dynamic and responsible governance of R&I.

Innovation research has yielded a large number of discussions and definitions of what innovativeness means (see Mačiukaitė-Žvinienė et al., 2014). A starting point can be in the notion that innovations are not the same as invention. Rather, the idea of making new combinations of existing parts is suggested as an essential characteristic of innovation, which is generally considered to be a process of introducing new inventions of some sort into the market (see e.g. Tidd et al., 2001, p. 38). Rogers (1995), for example, defined innovation as

> an idea, practice or object that is perceived as new by an individual or other unit of adoption. It matters little [. . .] whether or not an idea is objectively new as measured by the lapse of time since its first use or discovery [. . .] if the idea seems new to an individual, it is an innovation.
>
> (Rogers, 1995, p. 11)

We largely share these basic remarks of the nature of innovations.

In the context of PE innovations, the question of innovativeness is more specific. It relates to the time and context of such activities; something is currently done differently in the context of governance than what was done before (Mallery et al., 2012). In other words, the question of innovativeness becomes a historical and perceptual matter, where the nature of current PE activities is being compared to our experiences and memories of the nature of past PE activities.

Two drivers for the changing practice of PE can be distinguished. First, there is the necessity to find more effective responses to the societal challenges and other problems of governance, such as decreased trust of decision makers or societal acceptance of technological solutions. Another driver can be found in the emerging opportunities provided by new information and communication technologies that provide new tools for the practice of governance, for example, crowdsourcing for the formulation of public policies, or citizen science for providing evidence of new phenomena and research issues that are important for the public at large or some local groups of citizens.

We are interested in studying innovative PE practices, since there is a high potential in them in solving some of the stubborn problems of R&I governance, including societal acceptance of technological solutions, limited democracy of R&I decision making, ineffective mobilisation of resources, limited awareness of technoscientific development and, at worse, irresponsible use of public resources. Innovative PE has the potential to help to address these and similar challenges of R&I governance better.

Box 3.2   Participatory performance

Participatory performance refers to the different functions of public engagement (PE), and to the scope and intensity of such activities.

Participatory performance

The concept of participatory performance was introduced by Rask, Mačiukaitė-Žvinienė et al. (2012). It was applied to study the scope and intensity of R&I policy debates in European countries. In that paper, the factors contributing to higher or lower levels of participatory performance were divided into *supply and demand factors* as well as *government policies* and *supportive factors*.

In sociological and political analyses of science in society activities, the levels and intensities of public R&I debates have been analysed by using methods such as media and policy discourse analyses (e.g. Gaskell and Bauer, 2001). In the PE2020 project, however, we took the challenge of analysing participatory performance in a completely different context, namely, in the context of research projects and programmes. In our view, the shifted focus involves an 'instrumental' and variegated perspective on PE. The reason for this is that unlike in SiS debates at a national level, in which an active culture of public debate can be considered to be an important goal in itself, this is hardly the case in the project and programme context. Instead, PE tools in these contexts usually serve both instrumental and specific purposes. Therefore, we have not aimed to build one 'block indicator' of participatory performance in a research project and programme context, but rather, we have chosen to explore and characterise the main performative functions of PE in such contexts.

Successfulness

> ## Box 3.3   Successful PE
>
> Successful PE involves the right people with the right methods and goals, while leaving a big 'footprint' on research, innovation and society.

In a paper on participatory performance in national contexts (Rask, Mačiukaitė-Žvinienė et al., 2012), we implicitly equated high levels of participatory performance (or broad scope and high intensity of public debate on science) with a successful culture of science in society. In the project and programme contexts, however, where the goals of PE are both more heterogeneous and specific, this assumption is difficult to justify. Since success (and failure) of PE is still in the interests of funders, policy makers and researchers, and since most PE managers reported about the successful aspects of their PE activities, we decided to elaborate our own definition of the success of PE. In doing so, we adopted a 'hermeneutical' approach, in which we included multiple criteria and iterative perspectives in the study of success factors. More precisely, to study the success of PE activities in research project and programme contexts, first we crafted a preliminary definition of success based on consortium members' own experience and insights. We enriched this conception with the ideas of the coordinators of the PE project studied, as well as with ideas presented in the evaluation literature. On the basis of these various components, in Chapter 8, we elaborate a synthetic model of PE evaluation to study the success of PE. Based on this model, we proposed a general but theoretically reasoned definition of successful PE (Box 5.1).

Dynamic governance

> ## Box 3.4   Dynamic governance
>
> Dynamic governance refers to the ability of policy making to handle issues in a rapidly changing environment requiring continuous adjustment of policies and programmes. In this framework, dynamic governance involves dynamic interactions between scholars, citizens, industry and government as an exploratory, inductive approach in setting performance standards for responsible research and innovation.

The dynamic governance framework conceptualises interactions between scholars, policy makers and relevant stakeholders in the context of multi-dimensional governance and actors, who influence on the performance of these programmes. According to Guldbransen (2014), the critical point is a presence or absence of dynamics, tension of changes and co-operation. Neo and Chen (2007, p. 8) defines dynamic governance as follows:

> Dynamic governance is the ability of a government to continually adjust its public policies and programs, as well as change the way they are formulated and implemented, so that the long-term interests of the nation are achieved. Dynamism in governance is essential for sustained economic and social development in an uncertain and fast changing environment, and in an increasingly demanding and sophisticated society where citizens are more educated and more exposed to globalization.

Building on Neo and Chen (2007), we acknowledge *anticipation, reflexivity* and *transdisciplinarity* among the key capacities that help policy makers to dynamically manage complex issues in modern R&I policy systems (see Figure 3.1). The dynamic governance framework pays special attention to the 'instrumental' role of PE, in other words, how PE can contribute to context wise, proactive, effective and efficient decision making – not only making science more democratic and ethically oriented. To balance the accelerated change caused by increasingly dynamic governance, we included *continuity* as an additional key capacity, also contributing to more responsible governance of research and innovation (see below).

Responsible research and innovation (RRI)

RRI is a policy concept, which has been supported by some recent academic research and reflection (Owen et al., 2012; von Schomberg, 2013; Sutcliffe, 2011). The concept is intended to provide a common policy framework for the development of more advanced forms of science governance in the European research area.

On one hand, RRI refers to the *responsible management of a wide range of sensitive issues related to R&I*, including open access, ethical issues, public engagement and gender issues. On the other hand, *RRI calls for developing a more anticipatory, reflexive and transdisciplinary orientation to research governance*. These aspects become clear from the two ensuing sentences to the European Commission (n.d.a) definition included in Box 3.5:

> RRI implies that societal actors (researchers, citizens, policy makers, business, third sector organisations, etc.) work together during the

whole research and innovation process in order to better align both the process and its outcomes with the values, needs and expectations of society . . . In practice, RRI is implemented as a package that includes multi-actor and public engagement in research and innovation, enabling easier access to scientific results, the take up of gender and ethics in the research and innovation content and process, and formal and informal science education.

Box 3.5   Responsible research and innovation

Responsible research and innovation is an approach that anticipates and assesses potential implications and societal expectations with regard to research and innovation, with the aim to foster the design of inclusive and sustainable research and innovation.

Dynamic governance and RRI

Dynamic governance and RRI are partly overlapping approaches, partly complementary to each other. Overlapping is the acknowledgement of anticipation, reflexivity and transdisciplinarity among the key governance capacities. For dynamic governance, however, such capacities are not merely to ensure responsibility, but rather, to achieve sustained economic and social development and other long-term interests of the nations and the EU. Yet, to ensure the responsibility of dynamic governance, which emphasises continuous adjustment of policies and programmes, an additional capacity may be required: the capacity to provide organisational and institutional continuity. Certainly, things change, and more rapidly all the time. But as has been recognised in the literature on PE and deliberative systems, without institutional continuity, isolated PE activities are not in themselves conducive to better governance (e.g. Parkinson and Mansbridge, 2012; Dryzek, 2010).

The key capacities in the model adopted here that are conducive to dynamic governance (anticipation, reflexivity and transdisciplinarity), are strongly connected with PE. Anticipation is a capacity that largely relies upon an early analysis and interpretation of the emerging orientations and practices of the key stakeholders, and this can mainly occur in a context of dialogue and consultation. The same can be said for reflexivity, which is not a personal capacity but is chiefly a collective product resulting from dialogue and exchange. Transdisciplinarity can evidently be practised only through a dense interaction between the various disciplinary communities.

PE also plays a pivotal role in contextualising dynamic governance. It is in fact quite evident that dynamic governance can be developed only through negotiations and consensus-building processes involving both internal and external stakeholders, allowing new practices to be fully embedded in a given institution or cluster of institutions. It is hard to imagine a contextualisation process without extended and continuous practices of PE and participatory mechanisms. PE can therefore provide indispensable support for shifting to dynamic governance, whereas the latter can offer new room for developing PE practices. In particular, dynamic governance is aimed at facing an environment characterised by wide and rapid changes, for which reason an effective collection of information about the changing environment is necessary. Such information is mainly gained through the interactions between the different internal and external players, who actually function as the main 'sensors' of the organisation. This goes in the direction of institutionalising and ensuring continuity to PE. Conversely, a non-dynamic organisation will likely frame PE merely as an ethical question or an optional practice to be occasionally carried out and not as an essential part of its own governance strategies.

4   Research questions

As discussed in the introduction of this volume, we will focus on three issue areas that are critical for an understanding of where the field of PE is developing (innovativeness), what the potential function of PE is as a tool for governing research and innovation (participatory performance), and how PE activities can be reliably evaluated (evaluation and success of PE). Corresponding with these issue areas, we define the research questions of this study as follows:

1   *Innovativeness – What are the characteristics of innovative PE?* We will address this question from several analytical perspectives, by using different analytical grids in the study of the 38 cases of innovative PE from our sample. The analytical grids applied include several categories of actors, PE tools and approaches, varied substantive, practical and normative outputs produced, as well as different strategies and approaches to institutional collaboration and societal influencing.

2   *Participatory performance – What are the performative functions of PE?* We will address this question in particular by focusing on how 'participatory performance' of PE can be measured in the context of research project definition and research programme development (as contrast to function of PE in some other contexts, for example, national debates on R&I)? We will also study the factors that can contribute to higher or lower levels of participatory performance in these contexts.

3   *Successfulness – How can the success of PE be evaluated and characterised?* In particular, we are interested in developing a synthetic model of PE evaluation that appreciates the various performative functions of PE, including a broader view of PE not merely as a tool for communicating science but as a tool for research governance and as an approach for inducing transformative change in R&I institutions.

The three broad issue areas do not only call for better academic understanding of the trends, functions and evaluation of PE innovations, but they also raise issues of practical relevance. How PE processes can be introduced to different contexts of R&I, and what resources and activities are needed for their successful introduction? To this end, we will also provide a short overview of the most repeated processual obstacles of PE processes, as well as some recommendations on how to overcome them.

Finally, in Part I of this volume we have described the broader context of this research, presented our approach, methods and data, and defined the research questions in focus. In the following Part II, we will report our findings of the 38 cases of innovative PE processes in terms of the above described research questions.

Part II

Results

Learnings from innovative
PE processes

5 Empirical data

What kind of cases are studied

This part of the volume presents the results of our analysis of PE innovations for the dynamic governance of R&I, based on the collected empirical data. The sample of 38 PE cases studied in this volume is truly a heterogeneous set of PE processes. Most of the cases are temporarily limited projects or programmes, but also other types of initiative are included, including a social movement, a legal framework and two types of organisational entity. Basic information about the cases is provided in Table 5.1, including the number of the case, title, coordinator, year and activity type.

The cases are from the years 1992 to 2016. The oldest example ran from 1992–1994 (*Imagine Chicago*, U.S.), while most of the cases are more recent, having been implemented during the period five to ten years ago, or they were still running during the analysis, in 2016. An example of an ongoing scheme is the *Flemish Science Shop* programme which has run for 20 consecutive years, and *Soapbox Science* initiative, which started as an experimental project in 2011, but has now turned into an international programme.

As regards the places, in addition to Europe where most cases are collected, there are three cases from the U.S. (*Imagine Chicago*, *Futurescape City Tours*, and *Empowering Citizen Voices in . . . New Orleans*). Three cases operate at the global level (*Let's Do It!*, *World Wide Views on Global Warming*, *Futurescape City Tours*), some two-fifths of the cases, respectively, operate at the European level (e.g. *CIVISTI*, *PARTERRE*), two-fifths at the national level (e.g. *G1000* in Belgium, *Citizens' Dialogue on Future Technologies* in Germany), and less than one-fifth either at the regional (e.g. *Law no. 69/07 of the Tuscany Region*) or local levels (e.g. the *Youth Council of the City of Espoo*, Finland). None of the PE processes was devoted to a single organisation or institution.

Some additional analytics on the cases, not fully included in this volume can be found in d'Andrea (2016). This includes, for example, information about the *types of target group*: lay people were targeted in 34 initiatives,

Table 5.1 Basic information about the 38 innovative PE cases: title, coordinator, year and type

N	Title	Coordinator	Year	Type
1	PRIMAS	University of Education Freiburg, Germany	2010–13	Project
2	Science Municipalities	Danish Science Factory	2008–11	Programme
3	Nanodialogue	Fondazione IDIS – Città della Scienza	2005–07	Project
4	Breaking and Entering	University of Copenhagen	2013–14	Project
5	EARTHWAKE	EUROSCIENCE	2007	Project
6	Let's Do It! – Movement and World Clean Up	Let's Do It Foundation	2012–18	Social movement
7	DEEPEN	Durham University	2006–09	Project
8	Flemish Science Shops	Vrije Universiteit Brussel and Universiteit Antwerpen	2003–ongoing	Programme
9	RESEARCH2015	Ministry for Science, Technology and Innovation	2007–08	Project
10	iSPEX	iSPEX consortium	2013–ongoing	Project
11	PERARES	Living Knowledge Network	2010–14	Project
12	SpICES	Atomium Culture	2012–13	Project
13	The Autumn Experiment	Vetenskap & Allmänhet	2013–14	Project
14	VOICES	Ecsite (European network of science centres and museums)	2013–14	Project
15	Societal Advisory Board	Joint Programming Initiative 'More Years Better Lives'	2012–Ongoing	Organisational entity
16	Imagine Chicago	Imagine Chicago	1992–94	Project
17	Bonus Advocates Network	BONUS programme	2010–11	Programme
18	Owela Open Web Lab	VTT, Technical Research Centre of Finland	Ongoing	Service
19	Citizens' Dialogue on Future Technologies	German Ministry of Research and Education	2011–13	Project

N	Title	Coordinator	Year	Type
20	GenSET	Portia Ltd	2009–12	Programme
21	Law No. 69/07 of the Tuscany Region	Tuscany Region	2008–13	Legal framework
22	Act Create Experience	WWF-UK	1996–ongoing	Programme
23	The National DNA Database on Trial	University of South Wales	2008–09	Project
24	2WAYS	European Science Events Association, Eusea	2009–10	Project
25	NanoDialogue	German Federal Ministry of Environment, Nature Conservation and Nuclear Safety	2006–ongoing	Programme
26	World Wide Views on Global Warming	The Danish Board of Technology	2007–09	Project
27	Bioenergy Dialogue	Biotechnology and Biological Sciences Research Council	2012–14	Project
28	Soapbox Science	Dr Seirian Sumner & Dr Nathalie Pettorelli	2011–ongoing	Programme
29	Futurescape City Tours	Consortium for Science, Policy & Outcomes	2012–14	Project
30	CIVISTI	Danish Board of Technology	2008–2011	Project
31	Empowering Citizen Voices in . . . New Orleans	America *Speaks*	2006–07	Project
32	Consensus Conference on Future Energy	Wissenschaft im Dialog GmbH	2010	Project
33	Peloton	Demos Helsinki	2009–ongoing	Programme
34	PARTERRE	Tuscany Region	2010–12	Project
35	Imagine Jersey 2035	States of Jersey and Involve	2007–08	Project
36	G1000	G1000	2011–12	Project
37	Youth Council Espoo	City of Espoo	1997–ongoing	Organisational entity
38	We the Citizens	University College Dublin	2011	Project

Note: The number of the case indicated in Table 5.1 is used both in the subsequent tables in this volume, and in the Catalogue of PE initiatives (Ravn and Mejlgaard, 2015), where the cases are fully described.

and respectively public officers in 18, stakeholders (i.e. individuals or groups involved with or having an interest in the issues dealt with in the PE initiative) in 15, experts in nine, researchers and academic bodies in eight, non-governmental organisations/civil society organisations (NGOs/CSOs) in two, and other entities in four cases.

We move on to report our analytical findings about innovativeness, participatory performance and ways to evaluate and measure success related to PE activities.

6   What makes PE innovative

Most of the PE processes studied were initiated by non-profit organisations such as NGOs, unofficial networks and associations, while research institutions were the next frequent promoters of PE, followed far behind by national governments and other types of institution (d'Andrea, 2016). If the non-public sector is therefore a strong promoter of this field, where is it driving this development? This is the issue that will be explored next.

As for the analysis of the innovativeness of PE activity, we report our findings concerning the following aspects (relevant subsections are indicated in parentheses):

* New ways of representation (6.1)
* Methodological and institutional hybridity (6.2)
* Focus on societal challenges (6.3)
* Bearing on political impacts (6.4)
* Other innovative tendencies in PE (6.5)

6.1 New ways of representation

In considering the key actors in research and innovation activities, academia and public authorities have traditionally had a strong role in the planning, implementation and evaluation of such processes. Public authorities represent the public sector, whereas researchers and research institutions have traditionally come from both the public and private sectors. In addition to these two sectors, the social sector – sometimes referred to as the 'third sector' – has in recent decades been increasingly involved in research activities by providing access to the interests and viewpoints of organised stakeholder groups, such as environmental and industrial organisations. The trend of increasing representation of the third sector is continuing strongly in many areas of R&I decision making, such as university boards and national research and innovation policy councils that involve members from such organisations (Rask, Mačiukaitė-Žvinienė et al., 2012). This is also reflected in our case studies, where the third sector is strongly represented.

Box 6.1   Fourth sector

'Fourth sector' is as an emerging field, composed of actors or actor groups whose foundational logic is not in the representation of established interests, but rather, in the idea of social cooperation through hybrid networking.

More recently we have witnessed the emergence of the 'fourth sector' which is becoming more prominent in many areas of public activity, not least in the context of R&I policy. There are several definitions of the fourth sector in the research literature. Sabeti (2009) refers to hybrid organisations, such as chaordic organisations (systems that blend characteristics of chaos and order),[1] social enterprises, cross-sectoral partnerships and community interest corporations. Williams (2002) refers to the world of volunteering and 'one-to-one' helping amongst affluent and deprived people. Mäenpää and Faehnle (2015) refer to public activism outside organised interest groups, such as neighbour self-help groups, local movements, pop-up restaurants and exhibitions, and small-sized cooperatives. Common to all these notions is that the fourth sector is seen as an emerging field, composed of actors or actor groups whose foundational logic is not in the representation of established interests, but rather, in the idea of social cooperation through hybrid networking. The four sectors are illustrated in Figure 6.1.

Figure 6.1 Four sectors of the economy and society

Our first observation about the sample of innovative PE processes is that the number and variety of players is high. This is illustrated in Figure 6.2, in which we clustered different types of actor around the four sectors just described. As the free-format shape of the figure suggests, allocation of the actors under the four sectors can only be made roughly. This is particularly the case with the fourth sector, within which we included the following subgroups: *hybrid experts* (e.g. 'gendered scientists' or 'science parliaments'), *randomly selected people, field experts* (whose expertise is not based on scientific expertise but on a combination of experience based expertise and systematisation of such experiences, as in the case of authorised gym instructors, see Väliverronen, 2016), and *life world experts* (whose expertise is gained through systematic organisation of experiences based on one's direct contact with the issues, as for example in the case of patient-activists, senior citizens and immigrants). It should also be noted that the border between the 'unorganised' fourth sector and the more organised groups representing the social sector is often blurred.

Figure 6.2 Different actors participating in innovative PE processes

Second, innovative PE is eager to involve the fourth sector. In the litera-ture on PE, the involvement of the fourth sector is often labelled as 'direct involvement of citizens', which is separated from 'stakeholder involve-ment' referring to the participation of the third sector organisations (Elson, 2014). We found that three-quarters (29/38) of the innovative PE cases directly involved citizens, either as the sole mechanisms, as for example in the *World Wide Views on Global Warming*, or more likely, as one of vari-ous involvement mechanisms. In any case, such active involvement of the fourth sector is in striking contrast to the 'state-of-the-art' in R&I policy making, where more traditional models of participation prevail.

Third, in most cases, the purpose of involving the fourth sector was to pro-vide a broad representation of socio-demographic diversity. This can be con-trasted with the intention to empower particular socio-demographic segments by targeting such groups or over-representing them in the samples. Highly different actor groups and societal segments were involved in the PE pro-cesses studied, as communicated in Figure 6.2. Youth were over-represented or targeted in one-third of the cases. Other systematically empowered groups included women (*GenSET*) and consumers (*Owela Open Web Lab*).

Fourth, random or stratified random sampling strategies were used in sev-eral cases (12/29) to control the selection of the participating citizens. Most of such cases belong to the category of 'public deliberation', which reflects the prevailing wisdom in the context of deliberative democratic theory and praxis to rely on 'micro-publics' as a means to provide access to unbiased arguments (Bächtiger et al., 2014). One-quarter (7/29) of the cases applied uncontrolled selection strategies, in which there was no intention to com-pose participating groups in any systematic manner. In some cases, this was understandable through the effort to maximise participation, as for example in *Imagine New Jersey 2035*. Most instances of uncontrolled selection, for example, *Soapbox Science* where passers-by can enter in a dialogue with senior scientists, belong to the category of 'public deliberation'. Other types included 'public activism' (*Let's Do It!*) and 'public consultation' (*Owela Open Web Lab*). Additional approaches to participant selection included self-selection methods (where a snow-ball type of processes is used) and mixed methods (see Appendix 2 online).

Fifth, the third sector (or stakeholder groups) was involved in most cases, including cases that were primarily oriented at citizen involvement. None of the cases were based only on expert representation, by involving only sci-entists or policy makers. One-fifth of the cases involved only stakeholders. Therefore, it is fair to say that an increasing involvement of the third sector is a long and still continuing PE trend in Western R&I policy.

Finally, innovativeness of participant representation reflects an increas-ingly systemic approach to the design of the deliberative processes. We found that in many cases, the strategies of participant engagement and representation were highly sophisticated. An example is the *Let's Do It!* campaign, for which separate involvement strategies were prepared for communication, political engagement, global activities and provision of know-how and support for the activists.

The following types of strategies were used in order to systematise participant recruitment:

- Recognition and reconciliation of the different rationales of participation. Examples of highly different rationales include experimentation (*Breaking and Entering*), co-production of knowledge, and comprehensiveness in representation of societal interests (*Social Advisory Board*). Different rationales imply different requests to participant selection and representation.
- The formal versus informal structure of the PE process. The nature of the structure implies different approaches to building and maintaining representation of politics and expertise. In more structured processes (e.g. *Flemish Science Shops*) there is the need to maintain clear division of tasks and responsibilities between different partners (e.g. professors ensuring scientific quality, CSOs identifying socially relevant problems), compared to some less formal processes (e.g. *Soapbox Science*), where the creation of random encounters between researchers and the publics is the key aspiration.
- One dividing line is whether stakeholders are being mapped systematically as in *Bonus Advocates Network* and in the *Peloton* process – or not so. Using such mapping methods steers PE processes toward models that are more systemic.
- Iterative versus event based engagement processes. Cases in which the engagement process was based on iteration (e.g. the *Deepen* project, for which focus groups were re-convened and represented in a final deliberation event) require a good understanding of the motivations and measures to attract reconvening participants in the PE process.
- On-line (e.g. *Citizens' Dialogue on Future Technologies, GenSET* and *PARTERRE*) versus face-to-face processes open up a whole set of issues on how, and how controllably, representation can be built into PE processes. More extensive reliance on web based methods increases the number of challenges on how to keep track of the virtually ramifying deliberations.

Overall, we found that innovative PE cases involve highly sophisticated tools and approaches to ways in which different actors are motivated to participate, how deliberations are structured, how networks are created and maintained, and how productive interactions are generated. The complexities of such efforts are reflected in the 'focus and approach' cluster of the cognitive maps (see Appendix 1 online).

6.2 Methodological and institutional hybridity

In the catalogue of innovative PE processes (Ravn and Mejlgaard, 2015) we divided the 38 cases into five methodological clusters: public communication, public consultation, public deliberation, public participation and public activism (Box 2.1). This categorisation is based on a fusion of two classic models, Arnstein's (1969) 'ladder of participation', which pays attention to the different levels that political power assigned to the participants, and Rowe and Frewer's (2005) model, which pays attention to the different directions of information flows between sponsors and participants. Both formal (e.g. organised deliberation process) and non-formal (e.g. public activism) PE processes can be included in these categories. The allocation of the 38 PE cases across the main methodological categories is illustrated in Figure 6.3.

Our first observation is that *nearly half (18/38) of the cases are 'public deliberation' processes.* By definition, these are processes that aim to have an impact on decision making, not by assigning political power directly to the participants but rather, by communicating the results of deliberations to policy makers, who in turn, are expected to react and 'give an account' of the implications of deliberations for decision making. The second largest group (12/38) are public consultation processes, the primary purpose of which is to inform decision-makers about public opinions and viewpoints on certain topics. The third largest group is public communication processes, which aim to inform or educate citizens (five cases). In addition, two cases represent public participation (*Youth Council Espoo* and *We the Citizens*), where

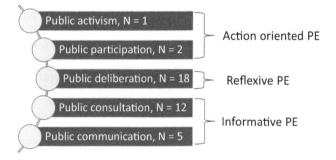

Figure 6.3 PE cases by main methodological category

decision-making power is partly or fully assigned to the citizens, and one case represents public activism (*Let's Do It!*).

Considering the role of the five methodological clusters in R&I decision making, we propose to use the term 'reflective PE' to cover public deliberation since such processes include several reflective functions, such as providing input, advice, feedback and evaluative insights from an expanded group of experts and stakeholders to decision makers. Following this logic, we propose to refer to public activism and public participation as 'action oriented PE', since they are oriented towards either making decisions or implementing them. Action oriented PE, in other words, is making decisions or implementing them – rather than merely debating about them. Finally, we refer to public consultation and public communication as 'informative PE', since their point is either to inform the public or decision makers about matters under consultation.

Our second observation is *'action oriented PE' is only marginally represented* (3/38), reflecting the status of the field more generally, at least in the sense that public participation processes where decision making power is directly delegated to the participants are rare few compared to other models of PE (e.g. Goodin and Dryzek, 2006). 'Reflective PE' (18/38) and 'informative PE' (17/38) were equally represented in this sample (Figure 6.3).

Third, *we consider the prevalence of deliberative processes to be an indicator of the increasing methodological maturity of the PE field.* Compared with traditional models of public communication and consultation, in which dialogue between decision makers and the public is narrow and restricted, public deliberation represents a more active model of SiS activity. This model is backed by recent ideas and theories of deliberative democracy that emphasise the importance of identifying relevant discourses and stakeholders and organising equal and inclusive discursive processes in order to reach agreements on complex policy problems (Gastil and Levine, 2005). The continuum of theory and praxis, embedded in the deliberative model, can increase the robustness, credibility and relevance of method development, which in the long run can help to consolidate the whole field of PE by providing scientific evidence for governance innovation.

Fourth, we found indications of *institutional ambivalence – simultaneous support and resistance – towards more innovative PE processes.* In other words, along with increasing methodological maturity, many of the PE processes were perceived as being risky interventions, and in many cases policy makers made qualified statements about them, which indicates that particularly 'reflective PE' can be perceived as threatening to existing practices of policy making (e.g. *Law No. 69/07 of the Tuscany Region, Act Create Experience, BBSRC Bioenergy Debate*). This reservation, combined with the fact that many of the PE processes studied were public consultation and public communication exercises in which the role of the public is even more limited, suggests that systemic scepticism toward innovative PE processes can easily cause them to slip back to more traditional SiS models.

Fifth, we found a comprehensive turn from one-way communication processes towards multiple-way communications. Rowe and Frewer (2005) characterised public communication and public consultation as 'one-way' communication processes, since in the former, information is expected to flow from the sponsors of PE towards the public, and in the latter, the expectation is the opposite. In our sample, we preliminarily included 18 PE processes in the category of one-way communication. Contrary to the expectation, however, we found that practically all PE cases (36/38) were based on two or multiple-way communication. Only *G1000* and *We the Citizens* (see Appendix 2 online), were classified as 'one-way' processes, since they both emphasise and try to protect the political autonomy of the deliberative panels, for which reason they to pursue limited interactions with such actors who might compromise their autonomy. Even in those two cases, however, we can still recognise a tendency towards multiple rather than a one-way flow of communications.

An illustrative example of the shift towards multiple-way communication is the *Nanodialogue* project. Its main aim (typically to a traditional science communication project) is to increase public awareness of nanotechnologies by raising curiosity and stimulating public debates on topical scientific issues. In reality, in contrast, the *Nanodialogue* project was a multidimensional communication exercise, in which a transdisciplinary group of philosophers, designers, politicians, social scientists, nanoscientists and members of the museum staff first co-designed the PE process; then they organised dialogues with families, schools, nanoindustries and science centres, which finally led not only to increased public awareness of nanotechnology, but also to a transformation of science centres' conception of their own roles in the business of science communication (from a spectator of scientific development to its active supporter). It would be a violation of the reality to label such activity as one-way science communication, since not only the public was targeted through educational efforts, but also the organising bodies whose identities were under revision.

Sixth, bold institutional hybridity is a clear sign of innovative PE. Institutional hybridity in our context refers to the mixing of traditional R&I policy institutions through PE processes. In general, we found that such mixing was high in terms of creating highly diversified networks of collaboration. We also found that highly diversified networks usually contributed to highly diversified outcomes in the PE projects. An example is *The Autumn Experiment* that involved schools, cities and researchers in a Swedish citizen science project: the results not only included registration and measurement of more than 2,000 trees and other scientific results but it also led to new teaching materials and methods for teachers, as well as to intensive public debates about the role of scientific research in Swedish municipalities. In particular, we found that the role of the following institutions is in a status of transformation through innovative PE processes:

- *Cities and municipalities* – these are among the main platforms of innovative PE processes. Even though smart city development is a well-known phenomenon that combines technoscientific development with city development, systematic strategies and infrastructures for science interaction at this level are still quite limited, even though there is much potential to benefit from them (see for example *Science Municipalities*).
- *Science centres and museums* – in many cases these adopted a stronger role in political influencing than is commonly considered appropriate for such 'neutral' players in the science policy arena. Examples include the *Nanodialogue project* focusing on understanding the transformative role of science museums, the *VOICES* project that involved a highly political process of defining strategic research priorities with regard to urban waste research in Europe, and *World Wide Views on Global Warming*, in which context some U.S., Japanese and German science museums facilitated dialogues about international politics of climate change (see Rask, Worthington et al., 2012).
- *Schools* – these were especially active in experimenting with citizen science processes that activate the whole network of actors related to primary and secondary education: pupils, teachers, parents, cities, service providers, scientists and regulators.
- Some of the more difficult to reach institutions – these included *international policy institutions* (e.g. UN COP negotiations in the World Wide Views process) and *criminal agencies*, as in the case of *the National DNA database on trial*, when young offenders were involved in a mock trial process in order to empower youth and local communities to deal with complex bioscience issues.
- *Business companies* – these are somewhat hidden in our sample of PE processes, but in a few cases, there have been promising results about the potential of PE in providing access to new product concepts and business ideas. An inspiring example is the *Peloton* process by Demos Helsinki, where an innovation platform was created to support environmental start-up teams to co-create new product and service concepts in collaboration with lead users and cities.

Overall, institutional hybridisation generated several types of win-win situations, by creating concrete platforms for co-design activities (cities and municipalities), transforming identities and core missions of R&I actors (science centres and museum), broadly mobilising communal resources (schools), mainstreaming policies (international negotiation), empowering marginalised actors (criminal political agencies) and stimulating creativity in product development (business companies).

Seventh, innovative PE uses multiple tools and instruments. We found that more than 20 mechanisms (out of the 76 identified in Ravn et al., 2014) had been used in our sample. Some of those mechanisms were used for the first time and they were unique, as for example 'Mock trials', 'Gatekeeper analysis', 'Co-creation spaces' and 'IMAGINE appreciate inquiry'. Four projects used the '21st Century Town Meeting' method (one of them was an 'electronic town meeting'); this was the most often used single mechanism in our sample.

Eighth, innovative PE processes combined face-to-face communication with electronic media. Almost all cases relied on face-to-face deliberation processes in establishing dialogues between the actors. One-fifth of the cases relied only on face-to-face communication, while the majority of the cases completed their communication with additional media, be it television, radio, phone, printed media, internet or other electronic applications (see Appendix 2 online). Electronic media were used in 70% of the PE cases including email, websites, blogs, podcasts, webinars, videoconferences, Twitter, Facebook, YouTube, SurveyMonkey, GoPetition, GoMeeting or other similar web-based applications. One-third of the PE cases used at least two types of media and every fourth of PE cases used three or more media to reach their target audiences. In addition to the internet, printed media were also popular. Almost one-third of the instigators of PE projects and initiatives reported that they used newspapers, magazines or posters.

We also explored the methodologies at a more general level, identifying most commonly used methods (see Appendix 4 online) and simply cross-examining how the use of such methods coincided with various features of innovativeness (see Appendix 6 online). The main finding is simple: *the higher the number of methods used, the higher the number of innovative features and impact on societal challenges* (Figure 6.4).

As Figure 6.4 indicates, the lowest number of reported methods was one while the maximum was eight. The average number of methods used per PE case was 3.5. All in all, the number of methods used relates highly with the innovativeness of the PE processes, which is understandable, since methodological mixing was one of our preliminary criteria of innovativeness. The numbers can be misleading however, as we could expect that one type of tool or instrument can actually contain several methods that were not just explicated in the case description. 'Media' for example, can include different types of media (TV, radio, printed and other types of traditional media)

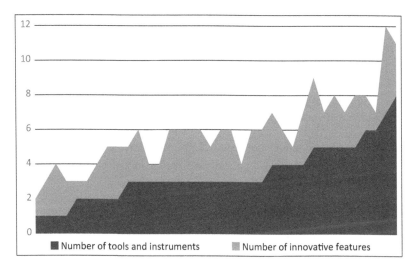

Figure 6.4 Coincidence of the number of PE tools and instruments with innovativeness (see Appendices 4 and 6 online)

even though this was reported as a single category. The simple statistic is still an indicator of the general trend that seems quite obvious: methodological mixing contributes to more innovative PE practices.

Ninth, as a corollary of the previous point, online tools and instruments were most often used as complementary methodologies. We found 16 cases in which online tools such as social media, websites, consultations, voting, emails, internet hearings and online debate portals were used in parallel with other methods.

Tenth, rather than being 'one-off' events, *many innovative PE processes are essentially systemic innovations*. Some of the cases may first appear to be single events, as for example the *Breaking and Entering* project that basically organised a physical installation on emerging applications of synthetic biology. On closer inspection, however, such processes reflect different types of boundary work across different domains, many times challenging existing norms and conceptions of the role of citizens, research, innovation and appropriate ways to communicate science in society. The following types of *institutional boundary work* could be found among the first ten PE cases:

- Multi-level policy communication – local, national, international (case 1)
- Multi-actor collaboration – public, private (cases 2 and 3)
- Multi-functional communication – science communication, scientific exploration (case 4)

- Transdisciplinary design – various sciences and practical expertise (case 4)
- Cross-sectoral dissemination – motivation of participants, global communication, provision of expertise, and so forth (case 5)
- Increasing organisational complexity, globalisation – strategic specialisation, spreading to more than 100 countries (case 6)
- Methodological iteration – local deliberative events, reconvened groups, final event (case 7)
- Historical continuity – 20 years of elaboration of the science shop approach (case 8)
- Political embedding – integration of the process in policy design (case 9)
- Expansion and programmatisation – widening and deepening use of the citizen science approach (case 10).

The list could be continued, but the point is evident: as recent scholars of deliberative democracy have emphasised, it is important to consider the systemic aspects of deliberative processes. This is becoming reality with the more innovative PE processes that we studied.

6.3 Focus on societal challenges

European research programmes reflect the policy priorities of the Europe 2020 strategies and address major concerns shared by citizens in Europe and elsewhere. In order to approach such concerns, European Commission (n.d.b) has defined seven societal challenges that orient research programmes and projects funded under the Horizon 2020 programme (Box 6.2).

Box 6.2   Seven societal challenges outlined by the European Commission

A   Health, demographic change and wellbeing;

B   Food security, sustainable agriculture and forestry, marine and maritime and inland water research, and the bioeconomy;

C   Secure, clean and efficient energy;

D   Smart, green and integrated transport;

E   Climate action, environment, resource efficiency and raw materials;

F   Europe in a changing world – inclusive, innovative and reflective societies;

G   Secure societies – protecting freedom and security of Europe and its citizens.

Orienting publicly funded research activities in addressing societal challenges – or grand challenges, as they are also called – is well justified due to their pervasive and compelling nature. Demonstrating that research and innovation activities are necessary to address societal challenges is also among the more powerful ways to legitimise public spending on European and national research programmes.

While the challenge-driven approach has obvious virtues as acknowledged by high level European strategies, there are also challenges in addressing the grand challenges, as Professors Stefan Kuhlmann and Arie Rip (2014) claim in their 'think piece'. The main challenge according to the authors is that addressing societal challenges involves an open-ended mission and requires systemic transformations. This is in contrast with more traditional R&I policies that focus on stimulating innovations in particular technological domains through dedicated funding programmes. To address societal challenges better, Kuhlmann and Rip (2014) call for a *tentative governance approach*, which includes ideas that governments should adopt a facilitative role in (a) orchestrating activities by a high variety of actors by creating new spaces for interaction – and actively involving new actors such as charitable foundations, which can operate with fewer bureaucratic and democratic constraints, (b) supporting experimentation through dynamic, provisional and revisable interventions, and (c) facilitating systemic change through tentative policy mixes. These three points (a–c) have been referred to here as the 'criteria of tentative governance'.

Against this briefly sketched background to societal challenges in European R&I policy thinking, what could be said about the potential of PE in addressing them better?

Our first observation is that innovative PE processes are widely oriented towards addressing societal challenges. Only one case, *We the Citizens*, was not classified as directly addressing societal challenges; even in that case, however, where the initiative aimed at 'showing the merits of random selection and deliberation in processes of discussing constitutional reform', we can see links to societal challenges, in particular Challenge F (*Europe in a Changing World*). In all other cases, PE processes were directly focused on addressing one or more societal challenges (Table 6.1).

Second, when addressing societal challenges, the level of ambition of innovative PE tends to be high. On average, each PE project contributed to three societal challenges. All seven challenges were addressed in seven cases, whereas only one challenge was addressed in eight cases. But the figures are perhaps less telling about the ambition levels. A better indicator can be discerned in the goal descriptions of the PE initiatives. *Let's Do It!*, for example, had the goal of 'cleaning up the whole world from illegally dumped solid waste' (relevance to challenges A, B, E, F); *Imagine Chicago*

Table 6.1 Orientation of the PE initiatives toward societal challenges

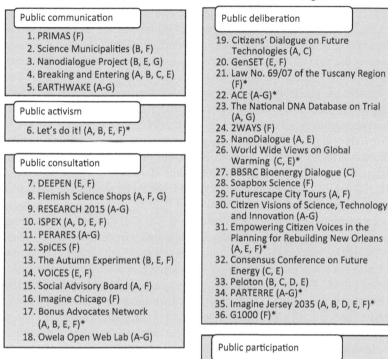

Public communication

1. PRIMAS (F)
2. Science Municipalities (B, F)
3. Nanodialogue Project (B, E, G)
4. Breaking and Entering (A, B, C, E)
5. EARTHWAKE (A-G)

Public activism

6. Let's do it! (A, B, E, F)*

Public consultation

7. DEEPEN (E, F)
8. Flemish Science Shops (A, F, G)
9. RESEARCH 2015 (A-G)
10. iSPEX (A, D, E, F)
11. PERARES (A-G)
12. SpICES (F)
13. The Autumn Experiment (B, E, F)
14. VOICES (E, F)
15. Social Advisory Board (A, F)
16. Imagine Chicago (F)
17. Bonus Advocates Network (A, B, E, F)*
18. Owela Open Web Lab (A-G)

Public deliberation

19. Citizens' Dialogue on Future Technologies (A, C)
20. GenSET (E, F)
21. Law No. 69/07 of the Tuscany Region (F)*
22. ACE (A-G)*
23. The National DNA Database on Trial (A, G)
24. 2WAYS (F)
25. NanoDialogue (A, E)
26. World Wide Views on Global Warming (C, E)*
27. BBSRC Bioenergy Dialogue (C)
28. Soapbox Science (F)
29. Futurescape City Tours (A, F)
30. Citizen Visions of Science, Technology and Innovation (A-G)
31. Empowering Citizen Voices in the Planning for Rebuilding New Orleans (A, E, F)*
32. Consensus Conference on Future Energy (C, E)
33. Peloton (B, C, D, E)
34. PARTERRE (A-G)*
35. Imagine Jersey 2035 (A, B, D, E, F)*
36. G1000 (F)*

Public participation

37. Youth Council Espoo (A, F, G)*
38. We the Citizens (none)*

Note: Cases indicated with an asterisk (*) are primarily focused on non-R&D themes. Cases without the asterisk are primarily focused on R&I themes. For the letters A–G, see Box 6.2.

aimed at 'cultivating hope and developing visions for a city and its citizens' (challenge F); *Law No. 69/07* aimed at 'developing Tuscany as a laboratory of deliberative democracy' (challenge F); and *G1000* had the goal of 'innovating democracy and letting citizens experience democracy' (challenge F). Needless to say, such goals are not intended to address the trivialities of societal change, but rather, they are to find new tools and remedies in addressing the wicked problems of our societies, such as polluted environments, and endangered democracy and social cohesion.

Third, in order to study the approach of the PE initiatives to the societal challenges, we divided the cases studied into two types: initiatives primarily focusing on R&I themes; and initiatives primarily focusing on other themes (Table 6.1). PE processes other than R&I focused were included in our sample, as the border between R&I and other themes is often vague. The case of *World Wide Views on Global Warming* is illustrative of this: its focus is primarily on climate politics, while at the same time climate change is only understandable through scientific theories and technological instruments. Further, this event was organised by the Danish Board of Technology Foundation (DBT), an agency specialised in supporting public debates on technoscientific issues. Examples of R&I-focussed initiatives include *PRIMAS* that aimed to promote inquiry in mathematics and science across Europe and *Flemish Science Shops* that supported dialogue between researchers and civil society. Examples of PE initiatives focusing on other themes include *G1000* exploring the future of the Belgian political system, and *World Wide Views on Global Warming* contributing to the international politics of climate change. While two-thirds of PE cases primarily focused on R&I themes, an interesting observation is that political framing dominated the two 'highest rungs on a ladder of PE', public activism and public participation, whereas public deliberation is a mixed category in which both R&I and other framings are present. Perhaps this reflects the fact that the closer one comes to decision making and action, the more political things get.

Fourth, we studied which of the seven societal challenges were addressed most often through the PE processes studied (Table 6.2). It was found that (F) *Europe in a changing world – inclusive, innovative and reflective societies* was the most frequently addressed societal challenge (28 cases), which is no wonder, since by definition, PE is about inclusivity. (E) *Climate action, environment* . . . (22 cases), and (A) *Health, demographic change and wellbeing* (20 cases) were the next two most frequently addressed challenges. Less attention was paid to the challenges (B) *Food security, sustainable agriculture and forestry* . . . (15 cases), (C) *Secure, clean and efficient energy* (13 cases), (G) *Secure societies* . . . (11 cases), and (D) *Smart, green and integrated transport* (10 cases). We have not made broad generalisations on the basis of our limited data, but we anticipated the low number of interventions targeted at challenge (G) *Secure societies* . . ., reflecting the fact that only belatedly had this challenge been included in the list of seven. We found surprising the limited attention paid to challenge (D) *Smart, green and integrated transport*, as sustainable transportation has been acknowledged as one of the more salient challenges in research by European citizens in past participatory processes. In the CIVISTI project, for example, development of attractive public transportation was considered to be the most important research priority by citizen panels in 7 EU member countries (Jacobi et al., 2011); in CASI-project, respectively, sustainable transformation of urban traffic infrastructure was considered among top ten research priorities by citizen panels in 12 EU countries (Repo et al., 2015).

Fifth, we analysed the extent to which the different categories of PE were applied to different societal challenges (Table 6.2). We observe that public consultation and public deliberation were the two main approaches applied

Table 6.2 Distribution of PE cases and categories per societal challenges

Societal challenge	Number of PE cases	Number of PE categories				
		Public communication	Public consultation	Public deliberation	Public participation	Public activism
A	20	2	7	9	1	1
B	15	4	5	5	–	1
C	13	2	3	8	–	–
D	10	1	4	5	–	–
E	22	3	8	10	–	1
F	28	3	12	11	1	1
G	11	2	4	4	1	–

with the most frequently addressed challenge, (F) *Europe in a changing world.* From the opposite perspective, public participation and public activism were rarely used approaches. Public communication and public consultation were used frequently, with the exception that challenge (D) *Smart, green and integrated transport* was addressed as a public communication exercise in only one case (*EARTHWAKE*).

Sixth, and returning to the discussion of Kuhlmann and Rip (2014), we found that innovative PE processes largely represent the 'tentative governance approach' in addressing societal challenges. They easily meet all three criteria defined above: (a) orchestration, (b) experimentation and (c) systemic change, as will be discussed next.

Seventh, criterion (a) – orchestration – is met in all cases, because, by definition, PE initiatives can be seen as complex orchestration processes. It should be noted that non-profit organisations are the main promoters of innovative PE processes (Table 6.3). As indicated in Table 6.3, there are also other types of organisation, which have promoted and orchestrated PE processes, including (in decreasing order of frequency) academic institutions, national governments, networks and local governments. Compared with the other types, non-profit organisations are therefore more inclined to see PE as a relevant way to address societal challenges. It should also be noted that some of the PE processes studied included large numbers of actors. The largest number and most varied of actors were included in the *Let's Do It!* campaign, which has operated in 112 countries and has included over 12 million participants. This example is a unique process, but it is worth remarking that there were many other initiatives that attracted thousands of participants. Examples include many of the citizen science processes studied as well as the international citizen consultation and deliberation processes, often subsidised by the EU. Overall, we want to underline

Table 6.3 Types of promoters of innovative PE processes

Type	No.
Non-profit organisations	14
Academic institutions	10
National governments	5
Networks	5
Local governments	3
Other	1
Total	38

the point that innovative PE processes are always challenging and multidimensional orchestration exercises.

Eight, criterion (b) – experimentation – is also frequently met, since many of the innovative PE cases were either methodological or socio-technical experimentations. *Breaking and Entering*, for instance, was truly an experimental science communication exercise. *The Autumn Experiment* was a large-scale experiment in citizen science, while *The National DNA Database* tested the mock trial method in helping young offenders to handle complex bioscience issues. Not all, but the majority of the PE processes studied included aspects of experimentation (and occasionally demonstration), in which sense they very much represent the idea of 'tentative governance'.

Ninth, innovative PE contributed to systemic change in multiple ways (criterion c). In some cases, systemic change was facilitated through new conceptualisations. *Science Municipalities*, for example, contributed to the notion of 'science municipality', while it also developed related infrastructure. Other examples of conceptual innovation include 'science parliament' (*2WAYS*) and 'long-term participatory foresight' (*CIVISTI*). Another way to facilitate systemic change was by building new competencies. *PRIMAS*, for example, focused on the promotion of inquiry based learning at both primary and secondary schools in Europe. New sociotechnical solutions were developed under several initiatives. Examples are *DEEPEN*, that developed solutions on how to govern a new domain of science (nanotechnology) under conditions of uncertainty, while enhancing innovation and remaining sensitive to public concerns. Resulting from this process was a new 'upstream' methodology that helped informing the EU's RRI policy about issues of nanotechnology. *Peloton* is another interesting case that developed an innovative way for citizens to participate in the co-creation of new products and services – and also contributed to the notion of 'smart-up'. Demonstration, finally, is a paradigmatic example on how systemic change can be promoted under the notion of 'tentative governance'. *VOICES* aimed at demonstrating that citizens' ideas, preferences and values can be taken into account in defining agendas for European research and innovation activities (in the area of urban waste). *World Wide Views on Global Warming* demonstrated that global citizen deliberation is feasible. *PARTERRE* focused on demonstrating the business potential of two new e-participatory tools. Figure 6.5 illustrates the four aspects of how innovative PE can contribute to systemic change.

Tenth, and finally, while innovative PE addresses societal challenges, we found that it is in no way immune to the impacts of the very same challenges. In particular, when PE processes are becoming more international and extensive in scope, they face the problem of how to manage cultural, linguistic and other types of requisite variety effectively (see, Rask, 2008). How successfully PE processes have managed to overcome such challenges is discussed in Chapter 8.

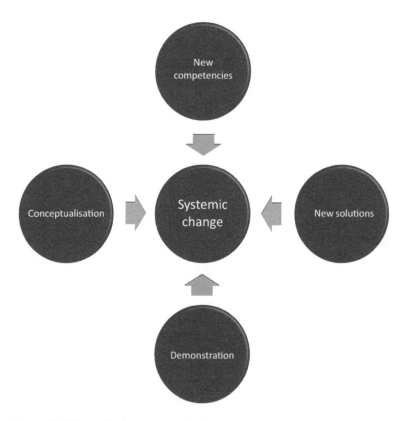

Figure 6.5 PE contributing to systemic change

6.4 Bearing to policy impacts

Bearing to policy impacts were considered a preliminary criterion of innovative PE, since limited policy impact of PE, especially deliberative minipublics, has been recognised by political scientists as a stubborn problem (see e.g. Grönlund et al., 2014; Kies and Nanz, 2013; Rask, 2013; Goodin and Dryzek, 2006). Bächtiger et al. (2014, pp. 225–226), for instance, state that 'to date, too few mini-publics have had a discernible impact on actual policy-making'. Remedies addressing this problem have recently been developed by the community of PE practitioners and scholars. One expression of this tendency is the current discussion on 'deliberative systems', which has shifted the focus from individual PE events to a consideration of the role of PE in a broader political setting (Rask and Worthington, 2015; Stevenson and Dryzek, 2014; Parkinson and Mansbridge, 2012; Dryzek, 2010).

The study of policy impacts of PE processes has often proved challenging for many reasons, including, for example, over-and under-determination of the impacts, long time spans between PE processes and related (or belated) policy processes, and the difficulty of defining, quantifying and measuring such impacts, for instance, changes in policy cultures, and empowerment of actors. While these are serious limitations of the study of policy impacts, we do not think that they should prevent us from entering in such a study, in particular, because the more public money is spent on PE activities, the more important it becomes to understand what their actual or potential payoff is. In addition, our data are highly expressive about the various outputs of PE, some of which we might appropriately call 'policy impacts'.

As we next continue reporting our findings about the policy impacts of innovative PE, we have emphasised that we are not establishing causalities, but instead, are reporting how managers of innovative PE processes perceived the outputs and outcomes of their activities. For example, the *Let's Do It!* world clean-up movement was claimed to have led to a rapid reduction of illegal dumping, and to an adoption of improved waste management practices in several countries. The PE2020 research consortium did not inspect the truth value of these claims against different data sets, but rather, it took these claims as the data, and analysed them to explore the nature and scope of policy impacts, by identifying emerging impact categories and trends, and reflecting on whether they can be linked to the different characteristics of innovative PE processes. This research strategy can claim to be 'uncritical'. In defence, we maintain that given the limited resources available, we preferred to invest in understanding the 'big picture' rather than inspecting the details. We also try to be explicit about this fact and encourage the reader to personally assess the plausibility of the findings.

Further, in order to analyse and describe the policy impacts of the PE processes studied, following conditions apply. First, we applied a broad definition of policy impacts. We started by analysing all types of the impact reported, and then proceeded to a discussion on different impact categories. Second, in order to organise the analysis of different types of impact, we applied the so-called TAMI model (Decker and Ladikas, 2010). This model, the name of which is derived from the project TAMI (Technology Assessment in Europe; between Method and Impact) was originally designed for the impact evaluation of participatory technology assessment processes, and it proved to be highly applicable, with minor modifications, to the study of the PE processes. The point of the TAMI model is to distinguish between three issue dimensions (scientific and technological, societal, and policy related aspects), and three impact dimensions (knowledge, attitudes, and action related aspects). We found it useful to keep the issue areas as such, but considered it a better fit to use slightly different categories for categorising the impact types. We ended up with substantive, practical and normative dimensions, reflecting the three main rationales of PE, as often repeated in literature on PE (e.g. Fiorino, 1990). Third, to sustain our discussion on innovative PE, we compared our policy impacts findings with some of the issues discussed before, including, for example, the role of the fourth sector, and focus on societal challenges. Finally, we remind the reader that an overview of the various outputs and policy impacts of innovative PE can be found on the right-hand side of the conceptual maps (Appendix 1 online).

Our first observation is that the impacts of innovative PE processes are truly diverse (Table 6.4). Scanning through Table 6.1, which provides a summary of the considerable variety in the various types of impact could be a pleasant surprise for a reader who might have expected PE to be a mere add-on to real R&I activities. Overall, we identified 55 different types of impact that were aggregated from 162 examples.

Our second observation is that most of the impacts of innovative PE can be described as practical. Following the TAMI model that distinguishes between three types of impact area – substantive, practical and normative – we found that 71% of the reported impacts could be allocated under the 'practical' category (Table 6.5). After making this bold claim, we make the qualification that in certain cases demarcation between different impact types was difficult. In most cases, however, it was rather easy to classify the examples. For example, *The Autumn Experiment* that contributed to 'scientific measurement and data' seemed clearly to be an example of how a citizen science project contributes to new knowledge by providing measurement and data on natural phenomena. More difficult cases were, for example, 'expansion and institutionalisation of PE' and 'conceptualisation' that we classified as practical impacts. 'Expansion and institutionalisation

Table 6.4 Summary of the impacts of the studied PE processes

	Substantive (e.g. new knowledge and ideas)	Practical (e.g. new products, practices, skills, social acceptance)	Normative (e.g. democratisation and empowerment)
Science & technology	Scientific measurement and data (13)	New products and services (1, 18, 33)	Expression of citizens' opinions of R&I (11)
	New scientific knowledge (13)	Methodological development and demonstration (7, 11, 14, 20, 23, 24, 26, 27, 29, 30, 34, 38)	Building consensus of R&I (9, 25, 32, 34, 35)
	Problem solving knowledge (8)	New educational contents and practices (1, 13, 22)	Confirmation of existing R&I policies (27)
	Research and publications (33)	Professional skills and networks (1, 5, 6, 8, 16, 19, 20, 26, 27, 28, 30, 33)	More responsible R&I (11, 25)
	University theses (8)	New solutions to societal challenges (6, 31, 33)	
	Academic debates (26)	Large-scale experimentation (21)	
	Knowledge transfer (8)	Fund raising for R&I (17, 31)	
	New research areas (14)	Conceptualisation (2, 3, 5, 11, 30, 33, 34)	
Societal issues	Crowdsourcing of new ideas (34)	Increased publicity (1, 4, 6, 8, 10, 12, 13, 17, 18, 20, 22, 26, 28, 31, 33, 36, 37, 38)	Empowerment of youth (16, 23, 37)
	Consumers' preferences and experiences (18)	Public awareness of environment (10)	Community building and ownership (16, 29, 31, 35)

(Continued)

Table 6.4 (Continued)

	Substantive (e.g. new knowledge and ideas)	Practical (e.g. new products, practices, skills, social acceptance)	Normative (e.g. democratisation and empowerment)
		Public awareness and debates of S&T (3, 4, 9, 12)	Increased local activism (31)
		Better understanding of scientific practices (13, 22)	Increased empathy and interpersonal skills (29, 31)
		Better image of science (10, 13, 24, 28)	More active civil society (6, 23)
		New models and platforms of collaboration (17, 18, 24, 33, 34)	
		New organisational functions (8)	
		Expansion and institutionalisation of PE (6, 8, 10, 11, 15, 27, 28)	
		Participant learning and behavioural changes (24, 32, 38)	
		Social innovations (14)	
		Social change (6)	
Political issues	Better understanding of public opinion (14, 26, 35)	Linking science and evidence to policy making (10, 20)	Policies driven by societal needs (11, 19)

Identification of regulatory implications (25)	Informing policy making (7, 20, 22, 24, 27, 30, 35)	Principles of deliberation introduced to legislation (21, 38)
	Policy recommendations (3, 5, 15, 19, 20, 26, 32)	Increased accountability of decision making (31)
	Parliamentary debates (10)	Democratisation of decision making (9, 37)
	New policies and regulations (20, 31, 37)	Renewal of democratic institutions (21, 36)
	Research agenda setting (14, 15, 17)	New governance skills and practices (6, 7)
	Allocation of research funding (9)	Trust and confidence in institutions (34)
	Promotion of challenge driven research (9)	

Note: Numbers refer to the 38 PE cases reported in Appendix 1 online.

Table 6.5 Share of different types of impacts in the studied PE processes

	Substantive	Practical	Normative
S&T issues	5%	27%	6%
Societal issues	1%	29%	7%
Political issues	2%	15%	7%

of PE' we decided to allocate in this category, as it seems neither to be about generation of new knowledge nor about realisation of certain norms, but rather about practices that are not so much scientific or technical, but are rather social (or to some extent political) in nature. 'Conceptualisation' in our examples was about many things, but most often it was about giving names, vocabularies or definitions to new issues related to R&I activities, be they a method of long-term participatory foresight (*CIVISTI*) or a concept of 'science municipality' (*Science Municipalities*). Other ways of classifying could have been possible, but we found that the current one best reflected the cases.

There is much talk about the rationales of PE: should it be driven by democratic, epistemic or pragmatic motivations? Our empirical finding is that innovative PE largely produces practical goods, such as increased publicity (18/38), methodological development and demonstration (12/38), and professional skills and networks (12/38). The two main issue areas where practical impacts were realised included social issues (29%) and S&T (science and technology) issues (27%), followed by political issues (15%).

Third, normative impacts including democratisation and responsibility of R&I are still important aspects of innovative PE, as almost half of the cases (18/38) reported of such impacts. 'Building consensus of R&I' (5/38), 'community building and ownership' (4/38) and 'empowerment of youth' (3/38) were the most frequently expressed impacts that we identified under the normative impact category. Although democratisation of research and innovation was a reported impact in only two cases, most of the normative impacts were related to it in one way or other, as is illustrated in Figure 6.6.

Fourth, creation of new substantive knowledge is not among the core outputs of innovative PE processes. We found only eight cases in which new substantive knowledge was mentioned among the outputs. The biggest category was new knowledge on S&T issues, which included five cases. In our view, only two cases contributed directly to new scientific knowledge. Typical for a citizen science project, *The Autumn Experience* contributed to new measurement, data, and finally new scientific knowledge published in academic papers. The *Flemish Citizen Science* project contributed to new 'problem solving knowledge and academic theses', and it facilitated knowledge transfer between academic and non-academic partners.

Figure 6.6 Normative impacts of innovative PE

The Europe-wide citizen consultation *VOICES* project contributed to the identification of new research areas. *World Wide Views on Global Warming* and *Peloton* – as two interesting and innovative PE processes – were targets of academic research and publishing, which was an indirect impact of these initiatives. Other epistemic impacts in the societal area included crowdsourcing of new ideas and revelations about consumers' preferences, and respectively in the political area, surveying of public opinion as well as identification of regulatory implications.

Fifth, *challenge oriented PE processes can stimulate impressive, socially and politically significant impacts.* We didn't possess a 'PE Richter scale' or other means to assign magnitude numbers to quantify the political impetus released by innovative PE processes. Instead, we observed that some of the PE processes had impressive impacts; or at least impacts that seemed to make a big difference in the existing political or societal order within the domains of environment (*Let's Do It!*), gender issues in research (*GenSET*), and municipal planning (*Empowering Citizen Voices in the Planning and Rebuilding of New Orleans*). The *Let's Do It!* initiative searched for and found new solutions to illegal waste dumping in 112 countries by mobilising over 12 million participants, including governments, CSOs and individual volunteers. *GenSET*, a multi-stakeholder dialogue project promoting gender equality in science contributed to the mainstreaming of gender issues in research activities, and to the introduction of related gender policies and regulations that are widely applied. *Empowering Citizen Voices in the Planning and Rebuilding of New Orleans* contributed to comprehensive rebuilding plans, and to the rebuilding of the sense of community after the city was devastated by Hurricane Katrina. Considering that one of these cases represents public activism (*Let's Do It!*) and the other two public represent deliberation, and that they all operate in different domains and political contexts, it seems that they may have limited commonalities. What we found combining these processes was a forceful focus on addressing real-life societal challenges: dealing with local environmental problems, reducing gender inequality in science, and rebuilding a devastated city.

Sixth, close to half of innovative PE processes enjoyed high media publicity. Media coverage can be considered to be an important element of PE, as for example in deliberative democratic theory, publicity is considered a necessary requirement for well-functioning democracy (e.g. Dryzek, 2000). In cases in which the role of media publicity was discussed, it was considered to be an important element in advancing public debates about R&I (e.g. *SpICES*), raising environmental awareness (e.g. *iSPEX*) and stimulating debate about new ways of exercising democracy (e.g. *G1000*). We found that all of the few cases of public activism and public participation stimulated high levels of media publicity. Half of the public consultation cases reported high media publicity, whereas only two-fifths of public communication and public deliberation stirred high media coverage. Despite online tools and social media having been used in 16 cases, their impacts were discussed only in one case, *Soapbox Science*, in which both traditional and new media were activated, and a large community of Twitter followers was formed, which contributed to the success of this programme.

Seventh, it should be noted that many of the innovative PE processes were oriented to exploring new methodological tools and approaches – not exploiting existing ones – for PE in S&T. *Breaking and Entering*, for example, was a thoroughly experimental science communication exercise, and for this reason, it didn't have ambitious goals to influence formal policy processes, but rather, it aimed to generate interaction and dialogue about the social role of science among festival visitors and contributing to public sense making of synthetic biology. Overall, we found that the more the PE process was oriented to methodological exploration, the less evidence there was of direct policy impacts. However, the border between explorative and demonstrative cases was occasionally difficult to draw, and if we look at the 12 PE cases that included 'methodological development and demonstration' (see Table 6.4), we observe that most of them contributed to some policy process by informing or making recommendations, and close to half of such initiatives were reported to be successful in this business. Among such projects are *GenSET*, the impacts of which have already been discussed. Other influential demonstration projects include *VOICES*, which developed a new transnational participatory process and influenced strategic research priorities of urban waste research in the EU; and *We the Citizens*, which piloted citizens' assembly in Ireland and integrated citizens' views at the heart of constitutional reform.[2] So, we have enough cases to draw the conclusion that *with proper project design an explorative orientation does not necessarily compromise the policy relevance of PE processes*, which should be an interesting finding for the proponents of 'tentative governance'.

Eighth, we found that *half of the innovative PE processes had an impact on governmental processes*. The following types of impact were identified. The least intensive way was *informing policy makers* and organising policy dialogues (cases 23, 30, 35). Occasionally this took place through *recommendations* (cases 5, 7, 19, 26). In two cases, the PE process led to *parliamentary debates*, including discussions on air quality in the Netherlands, following the *iSPEX* project, and summits hosted by the European Parliament on the theme of gender equality in science, stirred by the *GenSET* project. Three cases (25, 32, 34) contributed to *consensus building* and creation of agreement among policy makers and stakeholders. Four cases had a functional role in *allocating resources* to research activities (9, 14, 15, 27) and identifying lacunae in research priorities. For example, *Research 2015* directly contributed to the allocation of the strategic research funds in Denmark, and *BBSCRC Bioenergy Dialogue* reassured the UK Biotechnology and Biological Sciences Research Council about the direction the organisation is taking in terms of supporting bioenergy research. Three cases (31, 37, 38) contributed to *changes in regulation* by directly influencing policy making. For example, *Empowering Citizen Voices in the Planning for Rebuilding New Orleans* resulted in changes in key regulations of local governance, as antiquated zoning laws and master plans were updated, and the City Council and several city agencies codified citizen participation processes as an on-going part of local governance. Other examples are the *Youth council of Espoo*, whose duty is take part in decision making concerning children and young people, by making formal initiatives to the city board, and *We the Citizens* that informed the design of the Irish

Constitutional Convention, notably in having a random selection of ordinary citizens at the heart of this endeavour.

Overall, the listed categories of impact on governmental processes can be seen as a continuity in a 'spiral of participation' where informing and recommendation giving represent the initial steps, policy debating and consensus building processes make a move toward policy influence, which is finally implemented through the allocation of resources and change of regulations (Figure 6.7). We are not making the claim that PE processes that are tightly coupled to policy processes are more successful than other processes, rather, it should be acknowledged that such processes can result in a small-sized 'output footprint'. For example, the main aim and only reported outcome of the *Social Advisory Board* of the *JPI More Years, Better Life* was provision of policy advice, while the German *NanoDialogue* process was mainly focused on and resulted in an effective process of consensus building in the area of responsible use of nanomaterials.

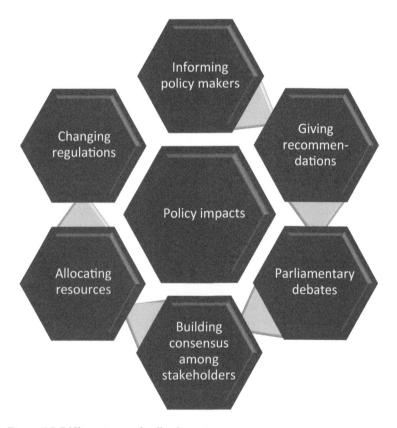

Figure 6.7 Different types of policy impacts

Ninth, an interesting observation is related to the different tendencies between European and U.S. impact orientations. While much of European PE is directed at influencing policy, the U.S. examples emphasise civic capacity and community building. *Imagine Chicago*, for example, contributed to community building by strengthening a shared sense of identity, helping appreciate understanding of other generations, and it contributed to youth development by providing them with empowerment, new competences, increased sense of ownership and leadership opportunities. *Futurescape City Tour* enhanced civic capacities through following elements: increased ownership, new networks and relationships, increased political efficacy, increased empathy, intrapersonal skills and skills in critical thinking. *Empowering Citizen Voices in the Planning for Rebuilding New Orleans* contributed to 'symbolic effects', including rebuilding the sense of community, restoring sense of connection, hope and community. Considering that we have only three examples (all in the field of urban planning) from the U.S., it is of course a strong claim to say anything about the differences between European and U.S. PE cultures, but since we found this tendency in all those cases, in our view, this suggests an interesting hypothesis for further study.

Tenth, there was a tendency for a gradual institutionalisation of PE. This can be seen as processes, where less formal and shorter-term activities transform to more formal and longer term activities. Important in this context is to distinguish between different types of activity that the PE processes studied represent. Two-thirds of them can be characterised as projects with a clear temporal limit, typically 1–5 years (see Appendix 7 online). One-fifth are programmes, usually involving longer time spans of 5–20 years. One-eighth are other types of activities, including, a societal movement (*Let's Do It!*), legal structure (*Law No. 69/07 of the Tuscany Region*), ICT-based service (*Owela Open Web Lab)* and two organisational entities (*Societal Advisory Board* and *Youth Council Espoo*).

We found that 27 PE cases had gradually developed towards more continuous activity schemes or programmes, or had been institutionalised in some other ways, such as establishing new concepts, methods, organisational structures, regulations, and infrastructures. The gradual institutionalisation of PE can be represented as a structuration process, in which ideas are first manifested as projects, which can then transform to programmes and structures (see Figure 6.8).

As Figure 6.8 suggests, social movements can also play an interesting role in the structuration process. Social movements can be effective in challenging existing structures and introducing new ideas. This was the situation with the *Let's Do It!* campaign, which started with some bold ideas on how to clean up a country in one day. As we found, the idea of *Let's Do It!* was first implemented as a national project in Estonia, which soon spread

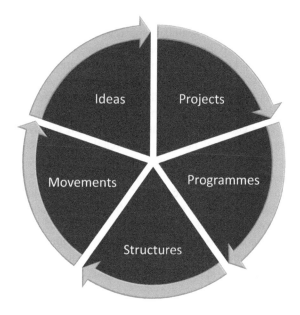

Figure 6.8 Structuration of the studied PE processes

to other Eastern European countries, and finally to more than 110 countries globally. Parallel to its geographical extension, *Let's Do It!* has been
transformed into a continuous programme, it has developed a sophisticated
organisational structure, and it was even granted the status of the United
Nations Environment Programme (UNEP) membership. Such a structuration process will inevitably change the identity of a spontaneous social
movement. This can perhaps be called a *'social movement governance
dilemma': while social movements are probably the most powerful form
of PE, they can hardly be managed through government actions without
losing their identity.* We are not suggesting that *Let's Do It!* would have
lost its power as a social movement; we only observe that it has become
more structured and in that sense its original identity as a spontaneous
social movement has changed. We also maintain that similar contradiction
is less pronounced for other types of activities, such as projects, as they are
often to some extent formal from the beginning. There were highly different
ways in which the PE processes studied had extended. *2WAYS*, for example,
covers approximately 30 European cities; *GenSET* has expanded to North
America, Africa, Asia-Pacific and Europe; *Science Municipalities* involves
25 out of 98 Danish municipalities; and *Imagine Chicago* processes have
taken place in specific neighbourhoods of Chicago and in towns and cities

around North and South America, Europe, Asia, Africa, and Australia. None of such cases reported of a decreased vitality, even though we observed some level of formalisation and 'structuration' taking place along with the geographic expansion.

6.5 Other innovative tendencies

So far, we have analysed characteristics and trends of innovative PE based on the pre-constructed criteria of innovativeness, discussed in Section 2.1. During the analysis, we observed some other tendencies that might become stronger in the future. These include the following trends:

> *Transferability* means the ability to transfer particular PE processes to other contexts and topics. This interlinks to the trend of the institution- alisation of PE, but also reflects the growing professionalisation and business orientation in PE activities. There are more and more consul- tancies and professional organisers of PE practices, who try to com- modify their PE tools and instruments. Sometimes it can merely be about the fact that good ideas can spread fast and virally. In many cases, however, the logic of commodification and expansion is strategic, and in many cases, this had led to regional, international or institutional transfer of PE practices. Among such PE cases we list *Science Munici- palities* and *ACE* that were transferred to other cities or regions of the country; *VOICES* and *SpICES* that were transferred to the European Commission's calls for proposals; and *iSPEX, GenSET, Imagine Chi- cago* and *Let's Do It!* that travelled internationally. The Danish Board of Technology foundation's two innovations, *CIVISTI* and *World Wide Views* processes have also been designed to be transferable. Elaborated applications of *CIVISTI* were designed and later used in other EU proj- ects (CASI, CIMULACT), and the global *World Wide Views* process has been applied both to new topics and new political scales, including regional, national and local processes.
>
> (see Rask and Worthington, 2015)

We already discussed the *use of multiple media* in the section on policy impacts, but a point should be made about the growing tendency to combine on-line tools and social media with face-to-face processes. The respondents to our survey asserted that the use of different media contributed to a better involvement of the public, induced wider discussion and increased aware- ness of the PE case.

An orientation to learning was clearly detectable in most cases, and it took several forms. In some cases, learning was an in-built feature of activities, as one-third of the cases were methodological development projects. Other learning functions included participant feedback, external evaluations, and scientific studies and evaluations. Award and prizes represent even broader societal scrutiny and recognition of PE activities. Such a strong learning orientation is not a self-evident fact, in particular, since there are pressures to make PE an everyday scrutiny for R&I actors. However, as we are here talking about innovative PE, there are several factors that contribute to an intense orientation to learning. Reflexivity and research orientation is in-built in the process of developing new methods and renewing related policy institutions. Programmatisation and institutionalisation also increase requests for financial and political accountability. Learning processes were seen as opportunities to move forward, improve activities through self-evaluation, observation and revision of PE practices.

Notes

1 An example of a chaordic organisation is Open Ministry in Finland (https:// avoinministerio.fi/), whose aim is to coordinate crowdsourced citizen initiatives. As anyone can propose and contribute to such initiatives, the content production is uncontrolled, while the Open Ministry facilitates and controls the process of preparation.
2 Irish Constitutional Convention is a participative democracy process in Ireland, tasked with considering certain aspects of the constitution to ensure that it is fully equipped for the twenty-first century and making recommendations to the Oireachtas on future amendments to be put to the people in referendums. The convention is a decision-making forum of 100 people, made up of 66 citizens, randomly selected and broadly representative of Irish society; 33 parliamentarians, nominated by their respective political parties; and an elected representative from each of the political parties in the Northern Ireland Assembly. See Arnold (2014).

7 What is participatory performance?

Participatory performance refers to the different functions of PE, and to the scope and intensity of such activities. For example, in the UK there are many professional and intermediary organisations providing PE services, as well as regulations and mechanisms contributing to a vital culture of science in society activities. Compared with some other countries where such institutions do not exist or are less developed, participatory performance of British R&I institutions can be claimed to be at a higher level (Rask, Mačiukaitė-Žvinienė et al., 2012).

Earlier we identified five categories of PE, including public communication, consultation, deliberation, participation and activism. All these categories point roughly to the different functions of PE: informing the public, asking them for feedback, organising deliberations between experts, stakeholders and members of the public, delivering decision making power to the publics, or mobilising activities through social movements. We have also identified issue areas in which PE can be relevant (issues such as S&T, social and political issues), and different types of political impact (substantive, practical and normative). While these categories are still useful in classifying PE processes and analysing their impacts, they are too rough to help understanding in which ways PE can contribute to various governance activities.

7.1 Focus on dynamic governance and RRI

In this section, we focus on the various participatory performance functions of innovative PE, by analysing such governance activities that emerged from the 38 cases studied. The analysis refers to the functional (left-hand) side of the cognitive maps (Figure 2.1 and Appendix 1 online). In particular, we have tracked activities that contributed to the four capacities of dynamic governance: anticipation, reflection, transdisciplinarity and continuity. Following Neo and Chen (2007), we have adopted a broad definition of these

concepts. Anticipation refers to foresight-type activities oriented at anticipating future development; reflection refers to public scrutiny of academic
findings or regulatory processes; transdisciplinarity refers to research and
planning processes that purposely involve not only researchers from different disciplines but also actors beyond academia; continuity refers to
activities that aim at embedding new activities in existing institutions or
otherwise building bridges between isolated interventions. We have given
more specific definitions in the following subsections. The most remarkable
difference to Neo and Chen's (2007) list of key capabilities of dynamic governance is that we replaced their notion of the 'capability to think across'
with the notion of 'transdisciplinarity'. We have also tracked other types
of activities and capacities, and analysed whether they were substantively,
practically or normatively oriented (Table 7.1).

It is important to study participatory performance in order to understand
the ways in which PE processes can potentially contribute to better science, better policy, and better SiS activities. In particular, our aim was to
understand how PE activities can support dynamic governance and RRI. In
order to support reflection on timely matters of European R&I policy, we
have also made a few observations on how PE processes might contribute
to open innovation, open science and the openness of European R&I institutions. These are the three strategic priority areas, proposed recently by
Carlos Moedas, the Commissioner for Research, Science and Innovation
(European Commission, 2015a).

7.2 Anticipation

Box 7.1   Anticipation

Anticipation refers to the capacity for prospective thinking and acting.

The faster the car, the further the headlights must go.
                                                                     —Gaston Berger (1957)

Anticipation refers to the capacity for prospective thinking and acting.
An antifatalistic, pre-active (anticipating changes) and proactive (pro-
voking changes) attitude is essential, as futurists Godet and Roubelat
(1996) have claimed, in the face of the accelerating pace of change, the
uncertainties of the future, and the increasing complexity of phenomena
and interactions.

Table 7.1 Participatory performance functions of innovative PE

	Anticipation	Reflection	Transdisciplinarity	Continuity	Awareness raising	Competence building	Action initiation
Substantive	Exploring impacts of societal change (35)	Identifying sustainable consumption choices (33)	Conducting transdisciplinary research projects (8, 10, 13)		Understanding public opinion (3, 12, 14, 18, 27, 38)	Educating democracy (37)	Piloting (2, 34)
Practical	Co-designing new products and services (18, 33, 36)	Publicly debating R&I issues (4, 12, 16, 17, 19, 20, 23, 25, 28) Increasing visibility of science in media (5, 12) Articulating public concerns on S&T (7, 29)	Designing transdisciplinarily educational programmes (1) Mobilising societal and financial resources (2, 5, 31) Testing new models of public-private partnerships (33, 34)	Expanding PE processes internationally (10, 11, 14) Creating enduring professional networks (1, 26)	Increasing public awareness of science (3, 4, 5, 10, 24) Increasing public awareness of environmental problems (6) Increasing awareness of gender issues in science (20)	Developing new competences for students (1, 8) Developing new competences for researchers (13, 28) Developing civic capacities (4, 29)	Mobilising citizens to clean their living environments (6) Introducing new 'science municipal' activities (2, 34) Building consensus and managing conflicts (25, 32, 35)

(Continued)

Table 7.1 (Continued)

	Anticipation	Reflection	Transdisciplinarity	Continuity	Awareness raising	Competence building	Action initiation
		Developing new methods for public reflection (24, 26, 27, 30, 34)				Expanding possibilities for science education in municipalities (2) Empowering youth (16, 22, 23)	Improving visibility and perception of women in science (28) Embedding citizens' values in local systems of innovation (29) Revitalising democracy (36) Influencing political processes (37, 38)
Normative	Developing future visions and plans (16, 31) Identifying future research needs (8, 9, 11, 15, 30) Upstream engagement (7, 8, 11, 14, 21)	Publicly debating regulatory issues (21, 26, 30, 32, 37, 38) Developing government accountability (31)	Aligning research activities with stakeholders (15, 17, 20, 23)	Institutionalising deliberative democracy (19, 21, 24) Establishing the use of PE processes in R&I governance (3, 6, 13, 15, 17, 18)			

Note: Numbers refer to the 38 PE cases reported in Appendix 1 online.

Considering the different performative functions of PE, anticipation of the future is among the core functions of innovative PE. This took place through participatory foresight activities and various collaborative processes identifying future research needs. Included in this group can also be so-called upstream engagement processes (e.g. *Deepen, Flemish Science Shops, PERARES, VOICES* and *Law No. 69/07 of the Tuscany Region*) that involve two-way communication at an early stage of the research or policy cycle, in contrast to downstream, in which selection instead of design is the key (see Joly and Kaufmann, 2008). Opening up the agenda-setting stage to a public- or stakeholder-based scrutiny can help anticipating and addressing such societal concerns that may become activated at a later stage of the R&I cycle.

7.3 Reflection

Box 7.2   Reflection

Reflection refers to the capacity to accomplish critical reflective dialogues publicly with relevant stakeholders, who can take the role of the other, develop shared values, and subject their reasoning to public scrutiny.

Reflection, in the context of our discussion, refers to the capacity to accomplish critical reflective dialogues publicly with relevant stakeholders, who can take the role of the other, develop shared values, and subject their reasoning to public scrutiny (cf. Raelin, 2001). Public reflection supports learning from past successes and mistakes, and it also helps building collective identities around focal themes and practices. Public reflection is also among the key concepts in the theory of deliberative democracy that promotes organising of public dialogues and deliberations around politically meaningful matters (e.g. Dryzek, 2010).

Public reflection on research and innovation is – by far – the most general function of innovative PE. While issues of R&I were the main subject of such debates, regulatory and policy issues were also frequently discussed. Different types of organised face-to-face discussion, events and workshop were the main participatory mechanisms used, while on-line tools were frequently used as supportive tools in close to half of the cases (17/38, see Appendix 4 online). Participants in the discussions involved experts and stakeholders, but increasingly also the 'fourth sector' as we reported in Section 6.1.

7.4 Transdisciplinarity

> **Box 7.3   Transdisciplinarity**
>
> Transdisciplinarity refers to the capacity of holistic thinking and acting by mobilising knowledge, expertise and other resources across and beyond scientific disciplines.

Transdisciplinary studies is a flourishing field of research, with its own university programmes and training schemes. Engaging in a full discussion on ways to understand the concept is beyond the scope of this volume, but we refer to Nicolescu's (2002) classic definition of transdisciplinarity, which refers to research activities that go between the disciplines, across the different disciplines, and beyond all disciplines. Ideas of holistically understanding the world and an underlying idea of the 'unity of knowledge' can also be found in literature (e.g. Klein, 2004).

Considering our data, transdisciplinarity is a widespread feature of innovative PE. Some two-thirds of the PE cases studied included at least some aspects of transdisciplinarity (Appendix 2 online), such as involvement of multiple disciplines in research efforts and challenge oriented definition of research priorities. As far as public engagement refers to the involvement of laypeople or non-experts in R&I activities, transdisciplinarity is even a tautological characteristic of PE. Yet we can observe differences between the ways in which innovative PE expresses transdisciplinarity. We found that transdisciplinarity is more tightly linked to the realm of policy rather than to research; to the transgression of established actor groups rather than to the transgression of scientific disciplines. One obvious reason is that our sample represents primarily innovative R&I governance practices, not innovative research practices. In line with this, most of the reported transdisciplinary activities included practically or normatively oriented functions, such as design of transdisciplinary research programmes, broad mobilisation of societal and financial resources for R&I activities and introduction of new public-private partnerships. Only in a few cases did we find instances of transdisciplinary research, for example in the citizen science project *iSPEX* as well as in the two cases of science shop initiatives (*Flemish Science Shops, PERARES*).

7.5 Continuity

Box 7.4 Continuity

Continuity refers to the capacity to embed new activities in existing institutions or otherwise building bridges between separate interventions.

Continuity is needed to balance accelerated change caused by increasingly dynamic governance actions. Conversely, if discontinuity prevails between different interventions and events, this hinders organisational and institutional learning and limits the effectiveness of interventions as there is no accumulation of the effects. The need for continuity has been recognised in various streams of the scholarly literature. 'Systemic turns' both in innovation studies (e.g. Smits and Kuhlmann, 2004) and studies of deliberative democracy (e.g. Parkinson and Mansbridge, 2012; Dryzek, 2010) both emphasise the importance of managing institutional interdependences and path dependences that can either support or hinder effective action.

PE, quite interestingly, is not in an arbitrary relationship, but is in a dynamic relationship with institutional continuity. On one hand, PE is often the change maker, by introducing new approaches to old governance dilemmas. In Figure 6.5 we illustrated how PE can stimulate systemic change by introducing new conceptualisations, new competencies, new solutions and demonstrations. In particular, introducing participatory mechanisms into the policy cycle may contribute to ensuring the continuity of dynamic governance. In fact, thanks to such mechanisms, the pace and scope of the policy cycle is no longer dependent only on the leaders of the organisations or on dynamics fully internal to the organisation. Indeed, PE may create a social pressure to the organisation forcing it to go on with the policy cycle and may make the process more transparent and accountable, so that it cannot be arbitrarily stopped or changed without any consequences (for example, in terms of reputation, credibility, and trust). On the other hand, externally developed tools and methods of PE threaten to remain disjointed from the actual practice of policy making, for which reason particular efforts are needed to ensure their relevance in the long term.

Continuity was an important aspect of the PE processes studied. Continuity was related to the aims to institutionalise the use of PE tools in R&I governance, and in some cases, to the institutionalisation of the principles of deliberative democracy in R&I governance, which is actually a highly ideological project. Along with these tendencies, a major proportion of innovative

PE processes have moved beyond a narrowly instrumental, methodological or event-based approach. In many cases, various types of 'boundary work' (Gieryn, 1983) were identified, including activities that aim to stimulate and manage interactions between different institutions, such as science centres, ministries and research institutes. As a consequence, innovative PE is not so much about providing researchers with new tools for effective science communication, but rather contributing to new skills and capacities to collaborate across institutional borders. As a result of such collaborations, we found enduring professional networks, internationally shared methodologies and guidelines that can help to further expand and consolidate the PE practice.

7.6 Other capacities

While we analysed participatory performance functions of innovative PE processes, we encountered activities that contributed to the four capacities of dynamic governance, but we also found functions that contributed to more 'able people' and more 'agile governance processes'. These are the two 'levers' of dynamic governance, as claimed by Neo and Chen (2007). Awareness raising and competence building are two functions of innovative PE that clearly contributed to more 'able people', while action initiation clearly contributed to more agile governance processes.

There is nothing surprising in the fact that awareness raising is an important function of PE, except that we are talking about a sample of the more innovative PE processes, which could be expected to move beyond the traditional awareness raising or 'enlightenment' paradigm (see Rask, 2003). This function is likely remain as a part of PE, since public awareness of R&I issues is a precondition of any other contributory function – be it epistemic, practical or normative – that members of the public may have, such as contributing to new scientific knowledge or taking part in making decisions concerning research funding. The interest in measuring public opinion and contributing to better public awareness of science are the two complementary functions of awareness raising activities.

Perhaps more interesting is to note that innovative PE processes contributed to new competencies, especially civic and democracy education and empowerment of youth. As the primary focus of our examples is research and innovation, this is a good reminder that such processes can be as important processes of democracy and youth education as more traditional educational institutions or political arenas. Getting involved in PE activities also developed new types of competencies for researchers, which is illustrated in *Soapbox Science*: researchers who participated in this process had fundamental career changing experiences.

We previously established in this study that public deliberation is the predominant category of innovative PE processes. As deliberation has often been described as a 'talk-centric' model of democracy (Chambers, 2003), it can be a surprise that *innovative PE has a major role in initiating action.* Piloting is among such functions, and we are talking about both the piloting of PE processes, but also what was piloted was a whole new infrastructure of science education and science deployment at the municipal level, as in the case of *Science Municipalities.* Most of the action initiating functions were related to the practical aspects of R&I activities. Such examples included consensus building and conflict management manoeuvres related to the themes of nanotechnology, energy policy and municipal planning, and mobilisation of citizens to clean their living environments (*Let's Do It!*). We also found cases in which PE processes directly influenced or even initiated political processes, as for example *Youth Council Espoo* that had the role of taking formal initiatives to city boards.

7.7 Open innovation, open science, open to the world

Open innovation, open science and openness of European R&I institutions are cultural factors that the Commissioner for Research, Science and Innovation Carlos Moedas outlined in his vision in an EU Conference on 22 June 2015 for a common EU approach to Open Science in Europe. In what follows, we have tried to estimate how innovative PE processes included such functions that can contribute to the three strategic priorities of European R&I activities (Box 7.5).

Box 7.5   EU's strategic priorities for open R&I

Open innovation is about involving far more actors in the innovation process. This can be stimulated by including an innovation-friendly regulatory environment, venture capital and by supporting excellence and promising companies.

Open science is about making scientific research, data and dissemination accessible to all levels of an inquiring society. This process can be fostered by opening access to research results and the underlying data – as well as by supporting research integrity that shows to the public that European science is above reproach.

Open to the World is about better science diplomacy and global scientific collaboration. This can be supported through collaborative projects, partnerships between regions and countries and taking leadership in addressing global challenges.

(European Commission, 2015b)

Table 7.2 Innovative PE processes contributing to opening of European R&I culture

Open innovation	Open science	Open to the world
Developing more favourable regulatory environment for nanotech (7)	Opening debate about risks and opportunities of nanosciences (3)	Mobilising research resources to support inquiry-based learning in European schools (1)
Innovating means to cultivate hope and civic engagement in Chicago (16)	Opening the secrets of synthetic biology to the public (4)	Providing access to regional resources to increase the quality of science education in municipalities (2)
Providing an online platform for open innovation (18)	Opening science through media (5)	Mobilising society and innovations to solve global environmental problems (6)
Assessing risks and opportunities of future technologies (19)	Opening research agenda setting (9)	Supporting collaboration between civil society and academia (8)
Innovating democracy (21, 35–38)	Involving the public in research making (10)	Supporting regional and transnational collaboration in research agenda setting (11)
Evaluating the risks and opportunities of nanotechnologies (25)	Involving the public in research activities (13)	Mobilising media to enhance Europe wide dialogue on science policy (12)
Engaging publics in strategy and policy development on bioenergy (27)	Formulating research agendas based on 'societal pull' (15)	Developing methods for research agenda setting at the EU level (14)
Engaging community members in local systems of innovation (29)	Raising awareness of gender issues in science (20)	Supporting macro-regional collaboration between national stakeholders (17)
Innovating means to rebuild a city (31)	Engaging youngsters in complex bioscience issues (23)	Providing youth responses to Earth Summit's global plan for environment (22)
Involving citizens in dialogue on future energy supply (32)	Supporting gender equal science (28)	Involving European citizens in two-way dialogue on life sciences (24)
Co-creating new products and services with start-ups and citizens (33)		Engaging citizens globally in climate policy debate (26)
Developing new eParticipatory tools supporting spatial and strategic planning (34)		Involving citizens in European R&I policy agenda setting (30)

Note: Numbers refer to the 38 PE cases reported in Appendix 1 online.

In order to reflect on how PE might contribute to the 'three O's agenda for open science', we analysed the main aims of the 38 PE cases and compressed main 'opening function' of each particular case in one sentence. As PE is fundamentally about opening R&I by involving new actors and perspectives, it was a simple matter to draw up such a list. The only problem was that the list could have been much longer. In a few cases the link to R&I was not pronounced (particularly in the five cases that primarily contributed to 'innovating democracy'). And in all cases the borderlines between open science, open innovation and 'open to the world' activities were blurry, but we prepared this table, more or less intuitively, to provide some topical commentary how PE can relate to this policy programme.

Many observations could be made about how PE contributes to the project of opening European R&I, but we have limited our discussion to a few remarks on the three openness dimensions mentioned:

As regards *open innovation*, we found several activities that involved far more actors in the innovation process, for example new platforms for open innovation, and engagement of members of the public in the evaluation of risks and opportunities of emerging technologies. In some cases, there were efforts to develop new regulatory frameworks to support responsible development of nanotechnology and new energy technologies. We did not find venture capital and measures to support excellence, nor promising companies.

As regards to *open science*, we found honest efforts to open up access to the public of complex scientific processes, which is not an easy task. This was done, for example, by organising experimental debates, participatory agenda setting exercises, and direct involvement in research activities through citizen science processes. Media and stakeholders were used to mobilize a two-way dialogue and the 'societal pull' perspective in science policy processes. Public evaluation or risks and threats of science, as well as gender equality processes, contributed an enhancement of research integrity. We did not consider projects that took open data as their primary focus, even though it had a role in several PE cases (*PRIMAS, SpICES*).

With respect to '*open to the world*', we found that an impressive number of the PE processes enhanced European wide collaboration, a few cases enhanced global collaboration, and many cases supported regional collaborations. Innovative PE, therefore, is very much about international science diplomacy (López de San Román and Schunz, 2017), creating collaborative efforts and enduring networks that can foster and spread new SiS practices in EU partner countries and beyond.

7.8 Measurement of participatory performance

Our research questions pertaining to participatory performance included a study of performative functions, but we were also interested in the problems of measurement and dynamics of PE processes through the following questions:

- How could we measure 'participatory performance' in the context of project definition and programme development?
- What factors could contribute to higher or lower levels of participatory performance in these contexts?

As we found, participatory performance, in this context, is a diversified phenomenon, for which reason there is no way to measure it directly at an aggregate level. Instead, it is possible to construct a composite model of several performance functions (see the next section), which could help orienting such a measurement. As a consequence, we expect that the only feasible way to analyse factors that contribute to higher or lower levels of participatory performance, requires focusing on the specific functions, such the role of PE in increasing capacities to anticipate or publicly reflect R&I policy issues.

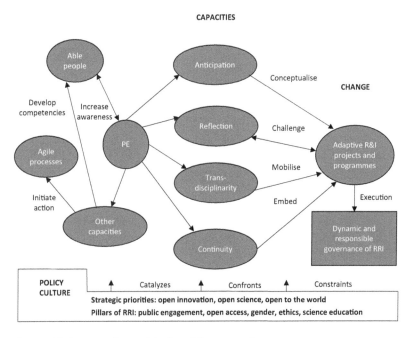

Figure 7.1 A composite model of participatory performance

7.9 A composite model of participatory performance

Summarising the previous discussion on participatory performance, we constructed a composite model that integrates the various elements and aspects just discussed: capacities, linkages between capacities, able people, agile processes and dynamic and responsible R&I policy, and policy culture, including both EU's strategic priorities related to openness, and the five thematic pillars underlying the EU's RRI policy – PE, open access, gender, ethics and science education (Figure 7.1).

Underlying Figure 7.1 there is the Neo and Chen's (2007) framework of dynamic governance that inspired the explorations of the PE2020 project. The format of the figure can therefore look old, but the content is new. It is our claim that such a holistic view of PE is unfortunately missing from today's research and innovation policy thinking. Yes, there is a desire to put PE more at the centre of research governance, but the vision has been blurred about the multiple conditions, capacities, linkages and requests that this programme involves with it. While this study has not provided answers to all these questions, at least it has contributed to a mapping of some of the key issues that need to be addressed in this endeavour.

8   How to evaluate PE

As PE activities increase in number and volume, it has become more and more important to evaluate the success of such processes. Actually, there are many types of evaluations which have reflected PE processes from different angles. The academic evaluation literature includes meta-evaluations (e.g. Beirle and Cayford, 2008; Dietz and Stern, 2008), theoretical discussions on relevant evaluation dimensions (e.g. Dryzek, 2009, 2010; Burton, 2009; Chilvers, 2008; Blackstock et al., 2007; Burgess and Chilvers, 2006; Goodin and Dryzek, 2006; Delli Carpini et al., 2004; Fiorino, 1990), academic handbooks (Gastil and Levine, 2005), as well as some more specific work such as studies of deliberative mini-publics (Grönlund et al., 2014) and European-level PE processes (Kies and Nanz, 2013). The literature targeted at practitioners include individual process evaluations (e.g. Warburton, 2011; Boussaguet and Dehousse, 2008; Goldschmidt et al., 2008; OECD, 2001) and toolkits that help to design new PE processes (e.g. d'Andrea, 2016, identified and compared 18 PE toolkits that are freely available on the internet).

In this volume we will describe a 'synthetic model of PE evaluation' that can help in targeting evaluations at the various functions and capacities of PE as a tool for dynamic and responsible governance of R&I. Reflecting on the discussions above, the key idea of this framework is to broaden the evaluation perspective from the habitual event and participant focused approach toward a more systemic view of PE, acknowledging also institutional impacts and indirect impacts, such as creation of spin offs that were frequently identified in our 38 PE case studies.

The model of PE evaluation will next be elaborated in an iterative process that includes the following four steps:

•   First, building on our own expertise and insight, we brainstormed a list of preliminary criteria that in our view characterise successful PE (Section 8.1).

- Second, an extended list of success factors was created by analysing how success was reflected by the managers of the 38 PE case studies (Section 8.2).
- Third, we introduced some classical project evaluation criteria (appropriateness, efficiency, effectiveness) that we used to review and complete our previous criteria (Section 8.3).
- Fourth and finally, we completed a synthetic model of PE evaluation by taking into account the rationales behind dynamic and responsible governance of R&I (Section 8.4).

Resulting from this process is the synthetic model of PE evaluation that consists of 40 key evaluation criteria classified into three main clusters (appropriateness, efficiency and impact), and nine subclusters. The following sections will describe the development of the success criteria, lists them, and present criteria for evaluations. The resulting synthetic evaluation model is presented in Section 8.4 and advice how to make PE successful in Section 8.5.

8.1 A preliminary list of success criteria

Defining criteria of success serves a dual purpose. First, it clarifies what can be realistically expected from (innovative) PE activity, or to put in the language of evaluation theory (Knowlton et al., 2013), what 'theories of change' are appropriate in the evaluation of PE. For example, our data suggest that different types of spin-off effects are widespread results of innovative PE processes, for which reason they should somehow be taken into account in the planning and evaluation of PE activities. Second, articulating potentially relevant success criteria can support development of such indicators that help to measure whether the intended goals of PE have been met. The following questions summarise the two different evaluation perspectives: first, 'is PE doing the right things?' and second, 'is PE doing things right?'

In order to start gauging factors that contribute to the success of PE, we organised a brainstorming session among the partners of the PE2020 research consortium. The brainstorming session was organised in January 2015 in a consortium meeting in Aarhus, Denmark, and it involved a dozen of PE researchers from Finland, Italy, Lithuania, Denmark and the UK. After brainstorming, clustering and ranking ideas, we arrived at the following preliminary list of success criteria (Table 8.1).

About half of the suggested criteria referred to the impacts of PE, while the other half pointed to procedural aspects. We named the two types of factors as 'preconditions' and 'outcomes'.

Table 8.1 List of ten preliminary criteria of successful PE

Preconditions	Outcomes
Balanced inclusion (6)	Improvement of policies, incl. effectiveness and responsiveness (4)
Transparency (4)	Enlarged capacities (2)
Motivation and reward (3)	Continuity (2)
Clear understanding of the objectives (3)	Efficacy (1)
Early intervention (1)	Acceptability (1)

Note: Numbers refer to the votes given by PE2020 consortium members to each criterion.

'Balanced inclusion' was considered to be the single most important criterion. The idea was that what matters most are the people involved, in other words, who will be selected to participate in a PE process largely defines its outputs and outcomes, as well as its democratic qualities. 'Transparency' and 'improvement of policies, incl. effectiveness and responsiveness' were considered to be the next two more important of the criteria. Transparency contributes to greater legitimacy of PE (while secrecy compromises it); transparency can also result from PE processes that publicly scrutinise decision making. Improvement of policies, increasing its effectiveness and responsiveness in particular, are two instances of the positive outcomes of PE.

Other criteria in the preliminary list include 'motivation and reward' and 'clear understanding of the objectives' – factors that help motivating people to participate and ensuring that they know what they are doing (informed consent). 'Early intervention' reflects the current 'upstream thinking' and related interest in opening up the decision process at an early stage of planning and decision making. 'Enlarged capacities', 'efficacy' and 'acceptability' cover both individualistic and institutional outcomes. 'Continuity', in turn, reflects the current 'deliberative systems thinking' and interest in embedding separate PE processes into the broader polity in a lasting way.

The preliminary list helped to consolidate the dual view of success factors, which also resonates largely with the PE evaluation literature. It also helped in articulating some initial ideas about successfulness that reflect current discussions about PE, including the high interest in advancing upstream engagement and developing deliberative systems. As such, however, the preliminary list proved to be inadequate in covering all relevant evaluation perspectives.

8.2 An extended list of success criteria

A broader list of potential success factors was generated by exploring the 38 PE cases: how PE managers described success in their own terms. As success was occasionally obvious but implicitly described, we also used our own wordings (e.g. PE processes had often travelled to dozens of new places, which was often reported merely as a matter of fact, even though it could be fairly described as a highly successful achievement).

An extended list of success criteria is presented in Table 8.2. Following the dual logic of the preliminary list, we distinguished between two categories of success criteria: 'procedural virtues' and 'utilitarian goods'. We identified three subcategories of procedural virtues: representative, value based and methodological; and in parallel, four subcategories of utilitarian goods: political, practical, institutional and substantive. Finally, we identified two criteria under each subcategory that in our view seemed most pronounced in the cases (in bold), and for the purpose of synthesising, we also included the preliminary criteria (in italics) in Table 8.2.

The extended list of success factors covers 74 criteria. While they all characterise what successful PE could look like, not all of them can be relevant in all cases. For example, access to European-wide public views might be highly relevant in some projects operating at the European level, but not in local level PE processes. While the extended list of criteria can serve as an inspiration for developing relevant evaluation criteria for the needs of the particular PE cases, we next created a short-listed set of 36 criteria with more universal applicability (Table 8.3).

The list is based on a number of highly varied empirical cases, for which reason it provides a rich spectrum of potential criteria, not limited to one particular aspect of PE, such as deliberative quality. We have the following observations about the procedural success criteria:

The three *representational criteria* (balanced composition, gender balance, wide representation of societal perspectives) are rather conventional, and refer to qualities that are expected from most PE processes. There can be instances where gender balance is not feasible, but at least the design of PE should be gender aware. Balanced composition is a kind of meta-criterion that needs specification, yet we argue that balance should be articulated in some way or other, and that the minimum requirement is that no particular interest should dominate deliberations (Renn, 2008). Wide representation of societal perspectives is a practical request for most PE processes, and as our cases have indicated, statistical or demographic representation is seldom necessary.

Ethical quality refers to the 'value based virtues', in other words, the value basis of the PE process. As a plurality of values is a fact of modern society, we find it unfeasible for PE processes to be anchored to some particular worldview, such as a philosophy or lifestyle supporting grassroots or business

Table 8.2 An extended list of success factors divided to 'procedural virtues' and 'utilitarian goods'

Procedural virtues

Utilitarian goods

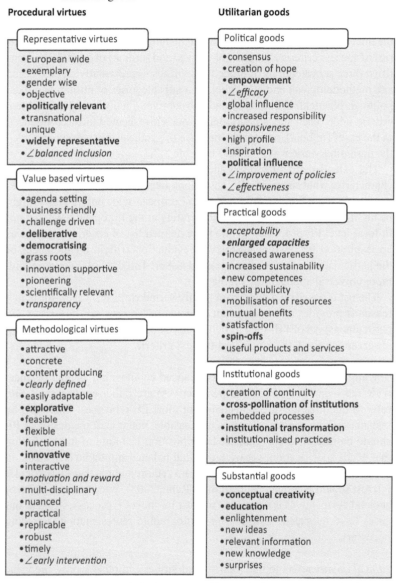

Representative virtues

- European wide
- exemplary
- gender wise
- objective
- **politically relevant**
- transnational
- unique
- **widely representative**
- ∠ *balanced inclusion*

Value based virtues

- agenda setting
- business friendly
- challenge driven
- **deliberative**
- **democratising**
- grass roots
- innovation supportive
- pioneering
- scientifically relevant
- *transparency*

Methodological virtues

- attractive
- concrete
- content producing
- *clearly defined*
- easily adaptable
- **explorative**
- feasible
- flexible
- functional
- **innovative**
- interactive
- *motivation and reward*
- multi-disciplinary
- nuanced
- practical
- replicable
- robust
- timely
- ∠ *early intervention*

Political goods

- consensus
- creation of hope
- **empowerment**
- ∠ *efficacy*
- global influence
- increased responsibility
- *responsiveness*
- high profile
- inspiration
- **political influence**
- ∠ *improvement of policies*
- ∠ *effectiveness*

Practical goods

- *acceptability*
- ***enlarged capacities***
- increased awareness
- increased sustainability
- new competences
- media publicity
- mobilisation of resources
- mutual benefits
- satisfaction
- **spin-offs**
- useful products and services

Institutional goods

- creation of continuity
- **cross-pollination of institutions**
- embedded processes
- **institutional transformation**
- institutionalised practices

Substantial goods

- **conceptual creativity**
- **education**
- enlightenment
- new ideas
- relevant information
- new knowledge
- surprises

Note: bold = most pronounced criteria among the 38 cases; italics = criteria emerging from the preliminary list; italics with ∠ symbol = links preliminary criteria under case-based criteria.

Table 8.3 Short-listed set of success criteria

Representativeness

- balanced in composition (no particular interests dominate)
- gender balanced
- widely representative of societal perspectives

Ethical quality

- deliberatively high quality
- democratically legitimate
- open (involves co-design practices)
- scientifically informed
- transparent

Methodological quality

- functional
- interactive
- motivating and rewarding
- practical
- robust (applies knowledge based practices)
- timely

Institutional impacts

- institutions renewing
- politically embedded
- practices transforming

Political relevance

- efficacy increasing
- politically empowering
- politically influential (e.g. improves policies, increases effectiveness of decision making)
- responsive

Practical impacts

- awareness increasing
- capacities developing
- mutually beneficial
- publicity increasing
- resources mobilizing
- satisfactory
- social acceptability increasing
- spin-offs creating
- sustainability increasing
- useful

Substantial impacts

- conceptually creative
- educative
- ideas generating
- knowledge generating
- informative

orientation. However, we find it justified that PE processes, at least to some extent, should reflect the values that are generally considered to lift the deliberative quality of communications. Such values include non-authoritarian aspirations including democratic legitimacy, openness, transparency and respect for scientific facts (e.g. Renn, 2008).

Methodological quality is composed of many different aspects related to the (professional) design of PE. In our view, the six criteria proposed cover some of the more fundamental methodological aspects of designing successful PE. More detailed lists of methodological issues could certainly be generated, based on years of accumulated methodological knowledge of best PE practices. However, such a list is not probably the best tool to support evaluations that also have to consider many other non-methodological issues.

We make the following observations about outcome or impact bound criteria:

Institutional impacts are evaluated only rarely, as it is considered that they take place over a longer time span than other impacts, such as participant learning. While this is often true, we found some interesting exceptions. Many innovative PE processes were actually targeted at transforming institutional practices, and quite often they were successful in doing so. Evaluation of PE processes, therefore, should take into account various types of institutional work carried out through PE. *Institutional renewal* refers to the introduction of new institutional structures or fusions between existing organisations and networks. This can be measured, inter alia, as the number of new networks and collaborative schemes stimulated by PE activities, for example, *Bonus Advocates Network* created new structures for research collaboration on Baltic Sea issues, and *Science Municipalities* contributed to new infrastructures for science interaction at the municipal level. *Political embedding* refers to the linking of the PE process to existing policy structures and processes. *Transformation of institutional practices* refers to the changes in the ways of managing issues and knowledge within an organisation. There is evidence that institutional impacts can occur even in the short run. For example, *GenSET* inspired gender summits supporting the preparation of research programmes, and actual societal and environmental change was rapidly stimulated by *Let's Do It!* The purpose of this study is to elaborate a set of relevant evaluation criteria, not to specify indicators that could be used in practically measuring success against the given criteria. However, in order to exemplify the issues that are related to such evaluation, we have also pointed to some relevant indicators. In this regard we also observe that awareness of new governance approaches usually precedes changes in them. An interesting way to measure the institutionalisation of PE is by asking participants to describe how they have communicated their experiences with other people. Warburton (2011), for example, found in the evaluation of the UK Sciencewise-ERC activities, that each dialogue participant is likely to talk to 30 others; this multiplied with by the number of Sciencewise-ERC participants during over the years (more than 13,000 people) means that some 400,000 members of the UK public have heard about their PE activities and related R&I themes.

Political relevance includes three types of criterion. First, empowerment and efficacy refers to the *increased agency of individuals* to take part in political and social activities. The concept of 'political efficacy' is a highly relevant concept here, referring both to beliefs about one's own competence to understand and to participate effectively in politics (internal efficacy), and to beliefs about the responsiveness of governmental authorities and institutions to citizen demands (external efficacy; see e.g. Craig et al., 1990). Many of our cases were targeted at youngsters, and political empowerment impacts were frequently reported in them. Second, *political influence* includes changes in the contents of policies and regulations. This can involve many things, such as new themes in parliamentary debates, changed research agendas, impacts on the allocation of research funding, promotion of challenge driven research, informing policy making, linking evidence to decision making, and policies driven by societal needs. Third, *impacts on decision procedures* include effects such as increased responsiveness of decision making and increased accountability of decision making, which is an often neglected but still an important aspect of responsible PE activity (e.g. Stevenson and Dryzek, 2014). As a distinction to 'external efficacy' that refers to participants' beliefs about the responsiveness of governmental authorities and institutions to citizen demands, here we are talking about actual acts of account giving by governmental authorities. The first aspect can be measured through polls, while the latter aspect requires a study of policy impacts. Responsivity, in this sense, should feature high in the definition of successful PE.

Practical impacts is another broad type of criterion, reflecting the finding that practical impacts are the most frequently occurring impact type in innovative PE processes (Table 8.3). Practical criteria can be divided into three subgroups. *Cognitive-attitudinal criteria* include increased publicity, participant satisfaction toward PE processes (some level of satisfaction is necessary to ensure that participants and stakeholders are willing to continue engaging in deliberative processes), and acceptability. As for the latter, we observe that there is a distinction between acceptance and acceptability. The difference is that acceptability refers to the attitude on R&I applications before their implementation, whereas acceptance refers to the attitude after their implementation (Schuitema et al., 2010). Harnessing PE to increase acceptance of already implemented R&I solutions can be democratically suspect, while finding ways to design more acceptable applications can be more easily justified. Quite interestingly, increased public awareness was not among the more pronounced success features, perhaps reflecting the fact that innovative PE is more orientated to other virtues, such as capacity building, networking and development of innovative types of SiS communication. *Competence-based criteria* include development of new capacities, spin-offs and practices supporting sustainable development, for example, effective waste management practices based on smart technologies in *Let's Do It! Resource-related criteria* include the creation of mutual benefits, mobilisation of resources, and instrumental usefulness (Table 8.3 provides further examples of each criterion; usefulness, for instance includes new products and services, methodological development, demonstration, and new solutions to societal challenges).

Substantial impacts, finally, involve a shorter set of criteria. This reflects the finding that substantial impacts belong to the least salient impact category of innovative PE (see Table 8.3). As evident in most of the cases studied, knowledge creation has not been the main point of PE, not at least creation of scientific knowledge. Rather, there are several examples of highly successful PE processes, in which knowledge production didn't play a role at all. Considering processes such as *Soapbox Science, Law No. 69/07 of the Tuscany Region, Let's Do It!, GenSET* or *World Wide Views on Global Warming*, all of them were impressive exercises in their own particular ways – in terms of *conceptual creativity, educational impacts and creation of information about public views* – but none of them was impressive in creating new scientific knowledge. Citizen science and science shops are among the few PE concepts in which creation of scientific knowledge is among the main targets. Even though contribution to *new scientific knowledge* has not thus far been a frequent aspect of most PE processes, it can potentially be highly relevant for the funders, organisers and stakeholders of PE, for which reason we have included it among the extended list of evaluation criteria.

In summary, both the extended and shortlisted sets of evaluation criteria complement the preliminary view of success through a procedural and impact oriented evaluation perspectives. In the following section we will finalise the synthetic model of PE evaluation by complementing and restructuring it with some classic project evaluation requests, including consideration of the *appropriateness* of PE.

8.3 Classic evaluation criteria

Classic criteria of evaluation, according to Georghiou and Keenan (2006, p. 769), include:

* *Appropriateness* – which refers to the question about the rationale of the activity, including consideration of the worth of public intervention and its alternatives. The latter includes reflection of the *additionality* (which is a counterfactual thinking exercise, asking whether the activity would have taken place without public funding).

* *Efficiency of implementation* – which refers to process evaluation focusing on managerial, organisational, logistical, methodological and other practical concerns.

* *Impact and effectiveness* – which refers to core issues of policy makers' concerns, namely to the outputs (measure of activity without measurement of its significance) and outcomes (activity including its significance) of PE activities.

Building on these classic evaluation criteria we start elaborating a synthetic model of PE evaluation, in which previously discussed categories of evaluation criteria are reviewed, and complemented with additional consideration of the rationales of PE.

Appropriateness

Evaluation of appropriateness covers two categories of criterion. First, having *appropriate goals* (A) is among the more important evaluation criterion, as it refers to the main aims of the PE process. For example, in the context of the EU's Horizon programmes, PE can be expected to contribute to more dynamic and responsible governance of R&I, as well as the EU's other relevant strategic goals delineated by the funder. It is perhaps relevant to note here that about one-third (13/35) of the European PE initiatives studied here have been directly funded by the EC or in the framework of EC-funded programmes (*PRIMAS, Nanodialogue, EARTHWAKE, DEEPEN, PERARES, SpICES, VOICES, Societal Advisory Board, Bonus Advocates Network, GenSET, 2WAYS, CIVISTI,* and *PARTERRE*).

Additionality refers to the additional value of investing public funding into an activity, which is one part of the consideration of the appropriateness of the activity. Second, publicly funded projects need to meet high *ethical quality* (E). In other words, they cannot be discriminating or misleading but rather, they must be based on openness, transparency, democratic legitimacy, and other similar values that reflect good governance principles.

As for the 38 PE case studies included in this volume, we can assume that their funders have already carried out some sort of appropriateness evaluation. To understand the inclinations in goal definition, we reviewed the goal setting of these processes. As an empirical finding, we found that *highly ambitious and general goals dominate over more modest and specific goals* (Figure 8.1). For example, *Let's Do It!* aimed 'to clean up the whole world from illegally dumped solid waste, and to support the most intelligent and sustainable waste management principles in order to ensure a future clean world'; *G1000*, respectively, aimed 'to be a citizen initiative that is capable of innovating democracy'; and *World Wide Views on Global Warming* aimed 'to give citizens an opportunity to express their views on some of the key issues negotiated at COP15 and engage policy makers in a dialogue about citizens' views'. In a few cases the goal setting was more modest and technically oriented, for example, *PARTERRE* aimed 'to demonstrate and validate the business potential of two novel eParticipatory tools for spatial and strategic planning in territorial development at the European level'.

Ambitious goal setting can result from the current tendency of policy makers to address societal challenges and support experimental policies. Actually, the salient role of the public sector, and the EC in particular, in funding innovative PE, resembles Mariana Mazzucato's (2015) vision that state has historically played a vital role as an active risk taker and funder of such research that has later resulted in important technological breakthroughs such as internet, GPS, touch-screen display, and the voice-activated personal assistant Siri in Apple iPhones. While highly ambitious solutions can be required to address societal challenges, also characterised as 'wicked problems' (see e.g. Australian Public Service Commission, 2012; Roberts, 2000), the downside is that this approach can lead to a distantiation from political realities, where solutions need to be practicable and connectable

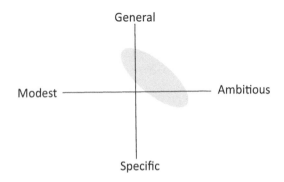

Figure 8.1 Main tendency of goal setting in innovative PE

to existing frameworks of action. An example is the *World Wide Views on Global Warming* method that has been criticised from losing connectivity between global policy question and participants' local experiences of environmental problems (Rask and Worthington, 2015). A related matter is that highly abstract goal setting can even hinder evaluation of PE processes, as it becomes difficult if not impossible to deem when the goals have been actually reached or not. For these reasons, it seems reasonable that even the most ambitious PE projects should contain some concrete and locally set targets that support practical orientation, learning from mistakes and refinement of better PE practices, based on evaluation and learning.

Efficiency of implementation

Efficiency means the ability to do things well, successfully, and without wasting energy, effort, money and time. It is important to ask whether resources have been spent both effectively and efficiently, since many of the PE cases studied have been large and expensive processes. For example, Rask et al. (forthcoming) analysed the budget of 20 transnational 'mini-public' type citizen deliberations that have been organised in Europe and globally. The budgets of these processes ranged between USD 400,000 and USD 6.9 million. The cost of 'one voice' (total budget divided by the number of participants) varied from USD 240 to USD 72,120.

Representativeness (R) or *involvement of the right people is perhaps the single most important issue contributing to the efficiency of PE.* While it is important to judge the composition of participants in PE processes, it is also important to note that PE often is the challenger of existing structures of governance. 'Crowdsourcing', for example, has proved an effective way of redistributing work previously carried out by public sector experts, as suggested for example by the successful opening of the U.S. patent review system to the public in 2007 (Howe, 2008). Crowdsourcing, citizen science and other similar forms of PE can also provide more efficient ways of gathering data, and in some cases even classifying it, than conducting the same activities by academic professionals. The point is that PE has much potential to save the energy, effort, money and time of public servants and research actors. Indeed, a systematic consideration of the potential of using PE as a tool to address inefficiencies in existing ways of organising research activities could pay back in multiple ways. Following this line of thinking, requesting all new EU research proposals to include an evaluation of the potential applicability of PE could pay back as well, and actually, such a scheme was successfully piloted in the context of the PE2020 project, in collaboration with the Academy of Finland, who introduced so-called societal interaction plans, where researchers where requested to make extensive plans of their SiS activities, and where the evaluation of such plans preceded scientific peer review (for further information, see PE2020, 2017). Having said that, it should be noted that involvement of the 'right people' is not only an issue of efficiency but also an issue of democracy.

Methodological quality (M) is another relevant factor contributing to the efficiency of PE. There is much practical and theoretical knowledge of the feasibility and functioning of PE methods, and our criteria are purported to reflect such insights. Functional, interactive, motivating, practical, robust and timely are just a few but highly important methodological characteristics that should be in-built in any PE process. Additional methodological 'rules of thumb' and design principles could be generated, for example, by building on the notion that 'one size doesn't fit all'. PE has to be tailored to the needs of particular socio-political contexts ('politically embedded' is a criterion in Table 8.3, which becomes closest to the aspect of context-wise design).

The capacity to sensitise different contextual requirements is to a large extent also a matter of *organisational competence* (O). The probability of success can be increased by having competent and well-resourced agencies organising the PE process. The data for this report were not particularly focussed on organisational aspects, but we acknowledge that they are an important precondition of successful PE, which could be further studied in other studies.[1]

Impact and effectiveness

For funders especially, it is important that PE projects meet their intended goals. Therefore, *goal attainment should be among the main criteria of successful PE*. Most, if not all, of the 38 cases studied can be classified as successful according to this criterion, which is no wonder, as we chose the 38 cases to represent most innovative and interesting PE processes, and we did not actively seek examples of failure. Even some of the most ambitiously oriented PE processes proved to be rather successful in this sense. *Let's Do It!*, for example, aimed to clean up the whole world from illegally dumped solid waste, and to support the most intelligent and sustainable waste management principles in order to ensure a future clean world. When looking at its achievements, *Let's Do It!* has rapidly helped reducing illegal waste dumping and introduced more effective waste management strategies in 112 countries (see Ravn and Mejlgaard, 2015; certainly, a closer critical examination of these impacts is warranted). *G1000*, in turn, aimed to be a citizen initiative that is capable of innovating democracy. *G1000* managed to organise an unprecedented grassroots political movement in Belgium (which was without government at that time) leading to the signing of the 'G1000 manifesto' proposing improvements to democratic institutions, and similar political mobilisation processes have later been organised in other parts of Belgium and other countries. *PARTERRE* is an example of a more modestly targeted PE process that aimed to demonstrate and validate the business potential of two novel eParticipatory tools for spatial and strategic planning in territorial development at the European level. Also, *PARTERRE* can be called successful, as it finally managed to quantify the benefits of the studied eParticipatory tools. More generally, perhaps reflecting the tendency of broad and general goal setting, we found that the impacts of innovative PE were quite broad, although with much variation.

Previously we proposed to categorise the impacts bound criteria into the following three clusters: *substantive impacts* (S), *practical impacts* (P) and *normative impacts*. This, combined with our previous classification of the topics of R&I policy in to three categories (science and technology, societal issues and political issues, see Table 6.1), would have neatly resulted in something similar to the TAMI model (Decker and Ladikas, 2010). While studying the 'normative impacts' more closely, however, we found it useful to divide such impacts (in Table 8.4) further into *institutional impacts* (I) and *political relevance* (Po). The reason is that institutional impacts refer to the changes in the structures of decision making, while political relevance refers to the PE processes and their relevance regarding political decision-making.

Overall, we observed that it is impossible to end up with a perfect categorisation, since in addition to the abundance of the types of issues and impacts, there are also many perspectives from which impacts could be regarded, ranging from individual to organisational and institutional. To address the difficulty of evaluating and classifying the impacts of PE in practice, in this study we relied on the *PE footprinting method* (see Appendix 1 online). Indeed, this technique proved to be useful in managing the complexity, and it can be recommended as a tool for practical evaluation and illustration of the key impacts of PE processes, for the following reasons:

- It is an easy, semi-structured approach to model and analyse categories of socio-policy impacts, for example, media coverage, impacts on policy making, participant learning, institutionalisation, enhanced civic capacities, new knowledge, new products, empowerment, mutual benefits, cultural change, community building, democratisation, societal change, and creation of professional networks.
- Being a semi-structured method means that while some of the more obvious impact types can be predefined, footprinting leaves room for the recognition of additional impact.
- Thus, including both predefined and particular types of impact, PE footprinting can reveal unique impact profiles for each PE case.

As most of our cases represent successful PE processes, at least in the sense of goal attainment, it is interesting to see that success can be achieved through highly different impact profiles. *Most cases studied were characterised by a broad impact profile* (e.g. *PRIMAS, The National DNA Database on Trial*), while in a few cases, the impact profile was quite narrow (e.g. *G1000, Societal Advisory Board*). Intuitively one could equate having a broad impact profile with being successful, and in parallel, having a narrow impact profile with being unsuccessful. What limits us doing so, however, is the observation that even limited impacts can stir deep changes in organisational practices and institutional structures. For example, the *Societal Advisory Board* of JPI More Year, Better Life, is doing pioneering work by introducing a mechanisms of societal peer review and practices of PE in the context of European Joint Programming Initiatives. Another example is *G1000* that introduced and helped to institutionalise practices of deliberative democracy in Belgium and other countries.

Publicity is yet another impact category which is relevant in the definition of different impact profiles. About half of the cases (17/38) reported high media publicity, whereas the other half (21/38) reported low or moderate publicity, or didn't report such impact at all. We did not find strong correlations between levels of publicity and impact profiles.[2] Instead, we can hypothesise that different orientations of the PE either support or hinder publicity. We assume that technically oriented PE (e.g. *Societal Advisory Board*)[3] and organisationally oriented PE (e.g. *The National DNA Database on Trial*) are less attractive to the media than politically (*G1000*) and societally oriented PE (*PRIMAS*).

In summary, considering what might count as successful in terms of sociopolitical impacts, we propose that *the bigger the footprint of PE, the bigger its additional value to society*. This idea is relative to the idea of 'social media footprinting', but PE footprinting covers a broader spectrum of activities (e.g. Rotsztein, 2013). A bigger PE footprint, therefore, can sometimes mean a broad or deep, or at best, both broad and deep imprint in society.

8.4 Synthetic evaluation model

Building on the previous discussion, in this section we complete the synthetic model of PE evaluation that can be used as a tool for targeting the evaluations at different dimensions (appropriateness, efficiency, impact), prioritising between (nine) categories of evaluation criteria and selecting the most relevant (among 40 different) evaluation criteria. As we previously argued, such a model can help to understand what can be realistically expected from successful PE processes and how the success of PE activity can be measured. Table 8.4 summarises the various evaluation perspectives discussed thus far.

Table 8.4 The synthetic model of PE evaluation

Appropriateness	Efficiency of implementation
A Appropriate goals • Goals relevant to dynamic governance and RRI • Coverage of other relevant goals • Additionality **E Ethical quality** • Deliberatively high quality • Democratically legitimate • Open (starting from co-design) • Scientifically informed • Transparent **Key components** • Right goals • Right principles	**R Representativeness** • Balanced in composition (no particular interests dominate) • Gender balanced • Widely representative of societal perspectives **O Organizational competence** • Skills and resources for designing and implementing PE **M Methodological quality** • Functional • Interactive • Motivating and rewarding • Practical • Robust (applies knowledge based practices) • Timely **Key components** • Right people • Right organisations • Right methods

Impact and effectiveness	
P Practical impacts • Awareness increasing • Capacities developing • Mutually beneficial • Publicity increasing • Resources mobilising • Participants satisfacing • Social acceptability increasing • Spin-offs creating • Sustainability increasing • Instrumentally useful **S Substantial impacts** • Conceptually creative • Educative • Ideas generating • Knowledge generating • Informative **Key components** • Big practical footprint • Big substantial footprint	**I Institutional impacts** • Institutions renewing • Politically embedded • Practices transforming **Po Political relevance** • Efficacy increasing • Politically empowering • Politically influential (e.g. improves policies, increases effectiveness of decision making) • Responsive **Key components** • Big institutional footprint • Big political footprint

Observing the synthetic evaluation model, our first observation is that PE includes a diverse set of activities, for which reason any single model can easily prove to be too restrictive. For example, some of the culturally oriented PE processes are not necessarily aimed at broad or deep policy impacts; however, even such processes will probably be aimed at some practical or institutional impacts, which is why it is important to acknowledge and accept a broad range of goal orientations. This has also been recognised among deliberation scholars, who have recently made a distinction between 'Type I' and 'Type II' deliberations (Bächtiger et al., 2010). Type I deliberations, according to Bächtiger et al. (2010, p. 36), focus on a deliberative process, emphasise rational, communicative discourse and orient to consensus, while Type II deliberation focus on deliberative institutions and outcomes, accept all kinds of communication (including rhetoric, emotional discourse, storytelling, and so forth), and welcomes different types of outcome, such as preference structuration, meta-consensus and increased intersubjective rationality. Type II deliberation therefore relaxes some established procedural quality criteria such as the request for sincerity. An up-to-date PE evaluation framework, in our view, should also become more relaxed and context-wise.

Second, the proposed synthetic model of PE evaluation results from an empirical study of a sample of innovative PE processes and reflection on the recent literature on PE. In order to increase the validity and relevance of the model, it has to be scrutinised (and publicly deliberated) with actors and stakeholders who are in a position to evaluate or appraise the potential value of different types of PE activities.

Third, even if this model manages to capture some essential insights of the dimensions of successful PE, it opens up a whole new body of work, along with the consideration of relevant indicators of each success criterion. Fortunately, much of this work has already been done, and indicators for deliberative quality, in the form of a discourse quality index for example, can be found in the academic literature as well as in practical applications (e.g. Lord and Tamvaki, 2013; Steenbergen et al., 2003). Some other criteria need additional reflection, however, for instance, the opportunity to acknowledge spin-off effects and other indirect impacts.

8.5 How to make PE successful

Defining and measuring success is a completely separate task from explaining what leads to success. To give an example, we have defined 'balanced composition' (a criterion in the category of representativeness in Table 8.4) as an important criterion of success, but we haven't explained how to reach such balance. Yet the question of how to reach success in activities is of great interest to anyone who plans to organise PE activities. What makes

this question difficult to address is that, first, there are many balance requirements, including for example, gender balance, balance of socio-economic
backgrounds and representation of different discourses around the topic
under deliberation. Second, any of these requirements involve different
strategies and actions to ensure optimal balance. For example, in a study on
the role of gender in global citizen deliberations, Goldschmidt et al. (2015)
identified biases in the representation of female and male participants in
the composition of citizen panels in the *World Wide Views* process. To miti-
gate them, they recommend 'composite recruitment strategies' based on the
combination of random sampling, targeted sampling and self-selection, as
well as paying attention to the organisational missions of the coordinat-
ing institutions, since NGOs focused on democratic governance have been
more successful in recruiting women in the developing country context.
What can be concluded from his example is that much knowledge of the
details and professional experience in designing and implementing participatory activities is needed to make PE processes successful.

We do not have enough room to engage in a discussion on how to reach
success across all the 40 criteria of success defined above nor do we possess such complete wisdom. What we will do next is something more modest, namely, *we will look at the challenges and obstacles of organising PE
activities* and classify them according to the nine evaluation criteria categories introduced in Table 8.4. This approach was called 'the science of muddling through' by American political scientist Charles Lindblom (1959),
who argued that it is fundamental to any organisation to learn from even the
smallest mistakes to improve the situation.

Overall, 118 challenges and obstacles were identified in the 38 PE cases
studied (they have been clearly indicated in each of the 38 cognitive maps
included in Appendix 1 online). On average, there were three challenges per
case. In order to understand the nature of these difficulties, we carried out
content analysis of the challenges and clustered them into eight thematic
groups.[4] These clusters are described next, and we have pointed out how
they are related to the areas of success described above.

The biggest group of challenges was *capacity-based obstacles* (28/38).
This includes a range of managerial difficulties that were frequently (13/38)
reported. Examples of managerial challenges include managing conflicts
and strategising between participating actors and stakeholders, getting
companies to understand their strategic role in PE processes, selecting the
right types of stakeholder and maintaining fruitful communications with
and between them, managing the framing of problems, creating shared
visions of expected outcomes, ensuring productive interdisciplinarity,
balancing power differences, and balancing between project obligations
versus partners' autonomy. Right timing and scheduling of PE processes

was mentioned as a challenge in several cases (9/38). For example, links to ongoing policy processes were missing, time pressure was chronic, and scenarios were outdated due to economic recession even before the project had ended. Inadequate capacity to evaluate PE processes was also recognised as a problem (6/38). Such challenges included limited follow-up, lack of relevant indicators for the measurement of capacity building, inadequate forms of feedback and so forth. The capacity-based obstacles result partly from an inadequate organisational competence, partly from inadequate methodological quality in developing well-functioning PE processes.

The second biggest category of challenges was *motivational obstacles* (22/38). It was reported that it is particularly difficult to motivate the following groups to participate: youth, industry, teachers, business, and academia. Several reasons were stated, including scepticism toward PE activities, institutions and hidden agendas. Mobilisation of researchers was difficult in many cases (7/38), which was explained through multiple reasons including the challenge of orienting researchers to thinking about societal challenges and contributing to the co-creation of knowledge, scientists' time pressure as well as their own ways of understanding what constitutes high quality science (for instance, for many scientists, science is primarily gender neutral, for which reason there is no perceived need for gender balanced production of scientific knowledge). Other difficulties included high dropout rates and transforming short-term participation to long-term commitment. Appropriateness of PE is definitely the core issue in understanding the motivational obstacles: if PE was to be regarded as an integral part of research, it is hardly difficult to engage researchers in it, but if it is seen as an external activity, the situation is different. Lack of motivation results in difficulties in engaging the 'right people', while adequate organisational competence is required to overcome such difficulties.

Technical obstacles were frequently mentioned (20/38). Here we are referring to available PE methods and their efficient use. Problems included effective use of social media (poor awareness of ICT tools, public limitedly engaged in Facebook debates), ensuring an adequate number of participants, covering multiple topics in one day, limited thematic coverage of the panel, self-selection, organising tours, exclusion of people needing assistance, inadequate facilitation skills, logistics, representation, on-line debating, combining face-to-face with online, organising simultaneous debates, dependency on cloud free days, and dependency on certain phone models. Technical obstacles belong to the methodological 'engine room' of PE processes.

Low impact was recognised as an obstacle in fewer than half the cases (18/38). There were two sides to this problem. First, low awareness or absorptive capacity of decision makers towards the PE process was a regular issue (10/38). Sometimes this was caused by inadequate ties to decision making institutions. In other cases, it was caused by the scepticism of administrators, which in one case (*Law No. 69/07 of the Tuscany Region*) led to a situation that the new law supporting PE was mostly ignored by decision makers, even though some other actors used it proactively. Second, low impacts were linked to fuzzy or trivial results. In some cases, citizens' recommendations were just too general to attract policy makers' attention, while in other cases, results were too specific, leading to having an impact only on little issues. Considering the nature of the examples, they are characteristically issues related to the lack of political embedding and political relevance. In many cases such problems result from the difficulties in framing the goals of PE in an attractive manner, and making the PE process motivating and rewarding for the participating actors.

That funding is challenging is no surprise to anyone. *Financial and resource-based obstacles* were mentioned in less than one-third of the cases (10/38), even though we might have expected that they would always be a challenge. In particular, longer term funding for PE is missing. Volunteering can help in expanding activities, but it can be unpredictable, and therefore it requires monitoring and management of relevant performance quality standards. Even though resource-based obstacles were not among the most frequently mentioned, they are severe in quality, as lack of or inadequate funding soon realises as very practical problems on how to conduct PE activities, if at all.

Cultural obstacles were also mentioned in less than one-third of the cases (10/38). This was particularly the case with several transnational PE processes, in which different languages, cultural habits, and professional norms prevail. A particular aspect of cultural challenge in the area of PE includes the hostility of NGOs towards deliberative processes and bodies, as they see PE as a threat to their own role as representing the voice of civil society (in their study of the *World Wide Views* process, Rask, Worthington et al., 2012 proposed to build an alliance between the PE process and NGOs to overcome this problem). Sometimes hidden motivations of PE processes were suspected, and some of their ideologies, such as the orientation to co-creation of knowledge with citizens, seemed to be distant. More typical cultural obstacles were related to challenges of intercultural communication. *Cultural obstacles are essentially about communicating the 'ethos', or the goals, essence and legitimacy of PE to its key audiences and stakeholders.*

Accidental or environmental obstacles caused surprises in about one-sixth of the cases (6/38). Examples of such challenges include corruption of the political system, difficulty of finding female scientists in PE processes, hostile media and civil society groups publicly questioning the legitimacy of PE, and unfortunate regulation that hinders opportunities for delegating power to the people. *Accidental obstacles can pertain to any of the activity clusters.*

Deficit based obstacles were minimal. Participants' inadequate understanding of scientific issues or inadequate capacity to handle e-participation was mentioned as a problem in two cases. Therefore, the deficit thinking that has been a persistent issue and problem in the area of R&I activity (see e.g. Irwin, 2001), seems to be fading away within innovative PE processes. Deficit based problems refer here to a sound understanding of the nature of PE activity and the role of scientific versus lay knowledge there within. *As a problem type, it is closest to ethical issues* (E).

To sum up, the main challenges of PE are related to questions of adequate professional capacity, motivation, technical skills and political impacts. Looking at how the problems mentioned could be allocated to the different categories of success, the most repeated ones include methodological quality and appropriateness, followed by organisational competence, ethical quality and representativeness. These are the issue areas where the organisers of PE should be most alerted to, and in the spirit of Lindblom's science of muddling through, should try to learn from past mistakes.

Notes

1 Some relevant factors that can contribute to a flourishing culture of PE practices, such as networking between professionals, existence of a different type of brokerage institution, interchange between universities and practitioners, as well as existence of pioneers and 'champions' were studied in Rask, Mačiukaitė-Žvinienė et al. (2012).

2 We did some simple statistical calculations by counting the number of different types of impact and checking whether they correlated with media attention. As mentioned, we didn't find a strong correlation, but definition of broad vs. narrow impacts seemed a bit arbitrary for this purpose. In future evaluations, this issue could be explored more systematically.

3 Despite its name, *Societal Advisory Board* can be classified as 'technically oriented' PE in the sense that it represents a stakeholder-based governance innovation rather than a direct PE innovation involving publics or supporting public deliberation through mass media.

4 Actually, we had three partners that happened to carry out independent analyses of the challenges. The Italian group identified 10 clusters, the Lithuanian group 11 clusters, and the Finnish group originally 12 clusters; finally, the Finnish group aggregated the different categories and ended up with eight main clusters. While someone could take this as an indication of the inaccuracy of the political and social sciences, our take is that this time we have an even more robust classification as it has been considered by several independent analysts. (However, we acknowledge that a fourth analyst might propose yet another classification).

9   Discussion

What are the benefits and limitations of PE in developing better R&I activity?

Public engagement has become an important theme in the development of research and innovation activities in Europe and beyond. By setting PE as one of six thematic elements of responsible research and innovation (in addition to open access, gender, ethics, science education and governance; European Commission, n.d.a), the European Commission promotes fundamental changes in the way in which civil society influences – and is expected to influence – research activities. Promoting PE means giving more weight to citizens and stakeholders in the definition of research needs, in the critical reflection of current and future research priorities, and in the implementation of research and innovation activities. Reflecting the interactive and dynamic nature of PE, we can even claim that PE is the heart and spirit of responsible research and innovation: it opens practices of research and policy to the publics and stakeholders; it involves ethical principles that highlight responsibility, (gender) equality and democracy, as well as effectiveness and efficiency of public decision making; it explores new ways to inform publics about prospects and risks of technoscience, and it mobilises citizens' capacities to address societal challenges.

Europe is not alone in this process. The American Association for the Advancement of Science (AAAS), the world's largest general scientific society is also devising its PE policies. During the time we were writing this volume, the AAAS was preparing its own 'logic model of public engagement with science', which involved systematic work for the definition of appropriate visions and goals for PE, and consideration of relevant PE activities and inputs that are needed to reach desired outcomes from PE activity – outcomes such as the publics' trust in science, improved ability and comfort of scientists to convene relevant communities to deliberate scientific issues, and an increased motivation of research actors to conduce responsive research.

It has been the purpose of this volume to contribute to a better understanding of the characteristics, trends and impacts of innovative PE, to study its different performative functions and to develop a synthetic evaluation model. By analysing a global sample of innovative PE processes, we have drawn lessons from the state-of-the-art in the field, and developed conceptual models that are both intended to support evaluation of PE practices and put PE in perspective as an element of dynamic and responsible R&I governance. Such work is necessary, since a better understanding of innovative PE processes can contribute to a better capacity for R&I governance and to developing better strategies to address societal challenges facing societies.

Even though our objective has not been to delve into historical research, we observed that there has been a shift of PE from traditional models of public communication and consultation, in which dialogue between decision makers and the public is narrow and restricted, to public deliberation in which such dialogues are intensive and influential. This shift we regard as an indicator of the increasing methodological maturity of the PE field. Furthermore, the continuum of theory and praxis embedded in the deliberative approach can increase the robustness, credibility and relevance of method development, which in the long run can help to consolidate the whole field of PE by providing scientific evidence for governance innovation. Other categories of PE studied, including various forms of public participation and public activism, represent increasingly interesting approaches to the governance of R&I, yet experiences are limited to making firm judgements on their relevance and usability in this context.

Some earlier studies have paid attention to the limited impacts of PE, and criticised PE from the tendency of it remaining an 'intra-mural' exercise (e.g. Grönlund et al., 2014; Kies and Nanz, 2013; Rask, 2013; Goodin and Dryzek, 2006; Rip, 2003). Contrary to these studies, we found innovative PE to have truly diverse impacts, not only on research and innovation but also on environment, society, politics – and individuals. Prominent examples of the latter effects include political empowerment of youth and development of 'scientific citizenship', in other words, new understandings of the rights, duties and responsibilities of citizens in relation to science and technology (see d'Andrea, 2016; Irwin, 2001). PE stimulates such impacts by creating opportunities for mutual learning between scientists, stakeholders and members of the public.

Considering the different types of impact, we found that most of the impacts of innovative PE can be described as practical. Such impacts include cognitive and attitudinal changes (e.g. better awareness of environmental and scientific issues), development of new capacities (e.g. new professional skills, methods and platforms of collaboration) and mobilisation of resources for addressing scientific and societal challenges (e.g. research funding, political commitment, public awareness and social acceptance). A subcategory of practical impacts includes impacts on policy making (e.g.

development of policy recommendations, informing R&I policy making with citizens' viewpoints and joint definition of research agendas). Other types of impact included normative impacts, such as democratisation and increasing responsibility of research. Instances of normative impacts included consensus building, community building, political empowerment, increased gender equality in science and introduction of the principles of deliberative democracy to R&I governance.

Finally, we observed that innovative PE only limitedly contributed to new scientific knowledge. Considering that our primary focus has been on PE projects related to R&I, this can be seen as a disappointing result. However, there were important deviations to this pattern. Citizen science and science shops, in particular, emerged as new concepts that not only involve co-design but also co-implementation of research and innovation. Thus, instead of drawing the conclusion that PE is impotent in engaging the public in actual research activities, we pay attention to these and similar concepts that provide even radical potential in developing more engaging research practices.

In summary, PE can provide new tools and approaches for the development and renewal of R&I governance in Europe and beyond. Innovative PE expresses the spirit of both 'tentative governance' (Kuhlmann and Rip, 2014) and 'dynamic governance' (Guldbransen, 2014; Neo and Chen, 2007), in which solutions are explored through pilots and experimentation rather than by introducing deductively driven or ready-made solutions. In addition to an entrepreneurial spirit of risk taking, we observed that innovative PE has contributed to new capacities that help research actors to address societal challenges and complex governance problems better. Such capacities include, among others, anticipation, reflection, transdisciplinarity and continuity, which we included as the key capacities of dynamic and responsible R&I in our 'composite model of participatory performance' (Figure 7.1). We also reckoned that PE is supportive of the EU's strategic priorities related to the efforts to 'open up' European research and innovations processes. In particular, we found innovative PE to be effective in conducting international science diplomacy, creating collaborative efforts and enduring networks that can foster and spread new SiS practices in EU partner countries and beyond.

9.1 A vision of PE benefitting European R&I activities

Despite widespread and positive individual impacts of PE, an overall vision of PE activity has remained unarticulated. How can innovative PE ameliorate research and innovation activities, so expected in several RRI declarations? To correct this flaw, we propose the following vision of PE, which invokes answers to this question (Figure 9.1).

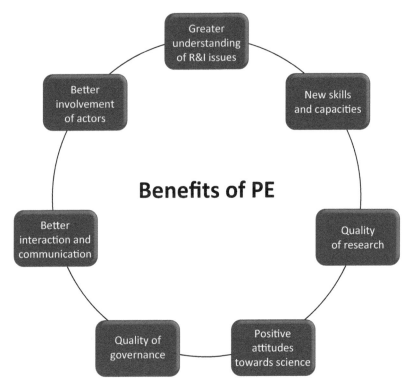

Figure 9.1 A vision of PE benefitting dynamic and responsible R&I activities

Our vision of PE benefitting dynamic and responsible R&I activities is built around the notion of better involvement of actors (see the box at 11 o'clock in Figure 9.1). Better involvement occurs, when 'right people' are gathered together to address 'right issues' through 'right PE tools and methods' (cf., Figure 7.1). While PE can be a rewarding experience in itself for the citizens, there is robust evidence of participant learning, indicating that through PE processes citizens can develop expanded understanding of the nature of the issues, as well as an increased sense of political efficacy, or a sense of possibilities to act on behalf of one's interests rather than feeling helpless and alienated from the reality. Even better, participation in collective problem solving efforts through PE processes helps citizens to develop new knowledge and skills that help them practically tackling even most challenging issues and problems (in *Let's Do It!*, for example, citizens were instructed to clean their living environments from toxic waste materials, and they effectively did so in more than 100 countries). The possession of new skills and capacities, in this vision, contributes to a better quality of research as more people are able to mobilise their experience and expertise in collective problem-solving efforts.

Unlike the infamous 'deficit model' (Irwin, 2001), in which provision of 'correct information' on science is expected to develop more positive attitudes toward it, positive attitudes toward science, in our vision are expected follow from a better quality of research. By better quality we mean research that has both academic quality and also ranks highly in 'societal peer review' (cf. Funtowicz and Ravetz, 2003), and which in addition to scientific expertise, also mobilises practical skills and societal capacities that are needed to address societal challenges and challenging research issues effectively.

Finally, like in positive psychology, which has established causalities between positive attitudes and better performance rates (e.g. Seligman and Csikszentmihalyi, 2014), we expect that a positive societal 'tune' can help to develop better R&I governance approaches, where public engagement, interaction and communication will remain among the key elements, as they have been defined in EU's RRI policies and its thematic priorities. – Following this logic, we have gone through a 'virtuous cycle' of PE, which is fundamentally our vision of PE benefitting European R&I activities.

9.2 Critical issues and further research

After contemplating a positive vision of PE, we end this volume by pointing to some critical issues that need to be addressed before the vision of PE benefitting R&I activities in Europe and globally could be fulfilled fully or partially. Some of the critical issues are related to the obstacles of PE, while other issues are related to the uncertainties of this business, pointing to further research needs. We also remark that there is a whole body of critical research on the problems related to PE activity, for example, (in)appropriateness of participatory models in different cultural contexts (e.g. Rask and Worthington, 2015; Einsiedel et al., 2001), (in)efficiency and (in)effectiveness as well as adverse effects of PE, such as 'political performativity' of PE rather than its political neutrality (e.g. Voß and Amelung, 2016; Felt and Fochler, 2010; Irwin, 2001; Levidow, 1998). Since the purpose of this study, however, has been more in *understanding the potential of innovative PE*, we have not this time delved into this important piece of literature.

Considering the potential of PE, an important critical issue is that compared to the high expectations, PE currently remains too weak to redeem its promises of increased societal relevance and high impact of R&I. In our study of the 118 challenges related to the implementation of the 38 innovative PE cases, we found that an inadequate capacity of the organisers of PE to manage complexities involved is the main challenge. Such complexities included effective selection of the participants, management of tensions between new actors, appropriate framing of the issues, and right timing of the processes, to name a few. A particular difficulty was an inadequate capacity to evaluate PE processes (this issue we have partly tackled by suggesting a synthetic model of PE evaluation). Other major challenges, in decreasing order of magnitude, included low motivation of the participants (often due to culturally bound ideas of appropriate roles of experts versus laymen in research activities), technical problems (e.g. inadequate facilitation skills and other hindrance of effective management of deliberations), low political impact, inadequate funding, cultural and environmental conflicts and finally, an underestimation of the capacity of the citizens to deal with complex issues (that was only a minor concern in our sample).

As the list of obstacles was gathered from a sample of the more innovative PE processes, we can expect similar problems to emerge in any pioneering organisation that starts to introduce PE in its organisational practices and structures. Therefore, it is important to acknowledge that many lessons have already been learned, and insights on how to avoid the worst pitfalls can be found in various places, such as the PE2020 toolkit (d'Andrea and Caiati, 2016) and dozens of alternative toolkits available on the internet (d'Andrea, 2016). The RRI tools (RRI Tools, n.d.) project provides perhaps the most topical site and resource for European PE planners of research activities, as this is a site that gathers together resources from all EU-funded projects in the field of RRI and PE. The results of PE2020 are also accessible on the project's web site through a design toolkit based on a 'critical approach', which acknowledges the inherent dilemmas of the PE practice, and suggests relevant solutions (d'Andrea and Caiati, 2016).

Finally, we remark that implementing dynamic and responsible research and innovation through a flourishing culture of PE is far from a finished project. The field is full of activities, experiments and ideas worth further clarification. We end this volume by suggesting a list of seven research questions, both academic and practical, that in our view deserve further attention:

We found that U.S. and European PE cases in our sample emphasised different virtues: while the U.S. colleagues are more interested in building civic capacities through PE processes, their European counterparts are more focused on policy impacts PE. *Are there notable cultural differences between U.S. and European PE activities, or is it merely a coincidence due to the small size of our sample that we found them?*

Funders of PE are interested in evaluating the economic impacts of PE, which is a fair demand considering the increasing volume of public expenditure in this field. At the same time, however, our experience is that none of the innovative PE cases studied directly aimed to create financial revenues, and if they did so, this happened indirectly.[1] To tackle this issue, we propose the following research question: *To what extent is it reasonable to model and evaluate the economic impacts of public engagement?* – Evaluation of the Sciencewise-ERC is one of the rare examples of evaluations that go far in the quantification of the impacts of PE (Warburton, 2011). For example, there is an estimation that each dialogue participant is likely to talk to 30 others about the PE process and its substance, which provides a basis for comparing the costs of communicating through PE versus other means. As for identifying other cost items, the 'footprints' of the 38 PE (Appendix 1, online) cases could provide a starting point for such consideration.

We found that three-quarters of the PE cases studied involved the 'fourth sector' (e.g. Williams, 2002) by including randomly selected citizens or other unorganised entities such as individual philanthropists and hybrid networks under formation. In this study, we identified four subcategories of fourth sector actor, including hybrid experts, randomly selected participants, life world experts and 'field experts'. To understand the challenges related to the participation of the fourth sector better, we suggest the following research question: *What subgroups belong to the fourth sector and how does their involvement have an impact on dynamic and responsible governance of R&I?*

We evidenced that 'upstream engagement' (e.g. Joly and Kaufmann, 2008) is an increasingly supported approach among innovative PE processes, especially in anticipatory projects. Upstream engagement aims to open decision processes at an early stage of agenda setting and planning. *Law No. 69/07 of the Tuscany Region* is perhaps the most extreme example of upstream engagement, as this is basically a scheme for supporting public deliberation on any issue that is proposed by the inhabitants of the Tuscan region; and if the issue is evaluated as being relevant by a competent authority, public engagement procedures will be financially and organisationally supported by the authority. To understand better the potential and limitations of upstream engagement for the governance of R&I, we suggest the following research questions: *What are the alternative models of upstream engagement that could be applicable for the governance of R&I? What are their main limitations?*

Creation of continuity was suggested as being an important capacity that is needed both to balance dynamic governance and sustain dynamism in the long run. We identified spatial, temporal and institutional dimensions of continuity, and acknowledged the recent discussion on deliberative systems (e.g. Dryzek, 2010; Parkinson and Mansbridge, 2012) to be supportive for building bridges between deliberative institutions links between separate

PE activities. As the arguments for continuity seem strong but the means to reach it seem unclear, we propose a study based on the following question: *What is the essence of the capacity to create continuity, and how can such capacities be developed in the context of PE activity?*

One of our findings was the highly limited contribution of PE to the production of scientific knowledge. At the same time, we acknowledge that citizen science and science shop activities have been highly successful in this area, and that they will most likely expand in the near future. What raises our curiosity are the following question: *Is there an untapped potential in co-creation of knowledge through public engagement? What could be the best means to support co-creation of scientific knowledge in future PE processes?*

The world of public activism is vibrant, and as our only case of this category, *Let's Do It!* suggests, there is considerable potential in it in accomplishing the tasks that we can expect from most successful PE processes. By using our own definitions of successful PE, we can clearly see that *Let's Do It!* has imprinted a big impact footprint in society, politics and environment; it has worked upon noble and widely justified goals, and from the point of the view of public policy, it has been extremely efficient, as the need for public subsidisation has been minimal. At the same time, public activism causes a dilemma for public policy makers: *What are the rationales, options and threats of harnessing public activism to serve dynamic and responsible R&I?*

Some of these questions can perhaps be banal for a social or political scientist who may have worked on these topics for years. For us, these questions are just a sample of some of the more intriguing dilemmas of public engagement.

Note

1 Resource mobilization, however, is an identifiable function of PE. It includes different types of activities, including fund raising (e.g. *Empowering Citizen Voices in the Planning for Rebuilding New Orleans*), matching innovators, startups and funders (*Peloton*), funding societally relevant research (*Flemish Science Shops*); most frequently it is about taking part in research prioritisation and allocation of research funds (e.g. *Societal Advisory Board, Law No. 69/07 of the Tuscany Region*). Examples of potential indirect economic gains include avoidance of costly societal conflicts over acceptance of new technologies, new ideas feeding innovation activities, and creation of new collaborative networks and platforms supporting research and innovation.

References

AAAS Center for Public Engagement with Science and Technology (n.d.). Why Public Engagement Matters. Available at: www.aaas.org/pes/what-public-engagement [5 Oct 2017].

Arnold, T. (2014). Message from the Chairman. Available at: www.constitution.ie/ [24 Aug 2017].

Arnstein, S. R. (1969). A Ladder of Citizen Participation. *Journal of the American Planning Association*, 35(4), pp. 216–224.

Association of Commonwealth Universities (2001). Engagement as a Core Value for the University: A Consultation Document. Available at: www2.viu.ca/integrated-planning/documents/Engagementasacorevalueoftheuniversity.pdf [5 Oct 2017].

Australian Public Service Commission (2012). Tackling Wicked Problems: A Public Policy Perspective. Available at: www.apsc.gov.au/publications-and-media/archive/publications-archive/tackling-wicked-problems [22 Sept 2017].

Bächtiger, A., Niemeyer, S., Neblo, M., Steenbergen, M. R. and Steiner, J. (2010). Disentangling Diversity: In Deliberative Democracy: Competing Theories, Their Blind Spots and Complementarities. *Journal of Political Philosophy*, 18(1), pp. 32–63.

Bächtiger, A., Setälä, M. and Grönlund, K. (2014). Towards a New Era of Deliberative Mini-Publics. In: K. Grönlund, A. Bächtiger and M. Setälä (eds.), *Deliberative Mini-Publics: Involving Citizens in the Democratic Process*. Colchester: ECPR Press, pp. 225–245.

Baumann, Z. (2000). *Liquid Society*. Cambridge: Polity Press.

Beck, U. (1992). *Risk Society: Towards a New Modernity*. London: Sage Publications.

Beirle, T. C. and Cayford, J. (2008). *Democracy in Practice: Public Participation in Environmental Decisions*. Washington, DC: Resources for the Future.

Bell, D. (1974). *The Coming of Post-Industrial Society*. New York: Harper Colophon Books.

Berger, G. (1957). Social Science and Forecasting. In: A. Cournand, ed. (1973), *Shaping the Future: Gaston Berger and the Concept of Prospective*. London: Gordon and Breach.

Beunen, R., Duineveld, M., During, R., Straver, G. and Aalvanger, A. (2012). Reflexivity in Performative Science Shop Projects. *Gateways: International Journal of Community Research and Engagement*, 5, pp. 135–151.

Bijker, E. W. and d'Andrea, L. (eds.) (2009). *Handbook on the Socialisation of Scientific and Technological Research*. Rome: River Press Group. Available at: www.scienzecittadinanza.org/public/SSERChandbook.pdf

Blackstock, K. L., Kelly, G. J. and Horsey, B. L. (2007). Developing and Applying a Framework to Evaluate Participatory Research for Sustainability. *Ecological Economics*, 60(4), pp. 726–742.

Boaventura de Sousa, S. (2010). The University in the Twenty-First Century: Toward a Democratic and Emancipatory University Reform. In: M. W. Apple, S. J. Ball and L. A. Gandin, eds., *The Routledge International Handbook of the Sociology of Education*. London and New York: Routledge, pp. 274–282.

Bok, D. (1984). *Beyond the Ivory Tower: Social Responsibilities of the Modern University*. Cambridge, MA: Harvard University Press.

Boussaguet, L. and Dehousse, R. (2008). *Lay People's Europe: A Critical Assessment of the First EU Citizen's Conferences*. European Governance Papers (EUROGOV) No. C-08–02. Available at: https://hal-sciencespo.archives-ouvertes.fr/hal-01066182/ document [26 Sept 2017].

Burgess, J. and Chilvers, J. (2006). Upping the Ante: A Conceptual Framework for Designing and Evaluating Participatory Technology Assessments. *Science and Public Policy*, 33(10), pp. 713–728.

Burton, P. (2009). Conceptual, Theoretical and Practical Issues in Measuring the Benefits of Public Participation. *Evaluation*, 15(3), pp. 263–284.

Caputo, R. K. (2010). Family Characteristics, Public Program Participation, & Civic Engagement. *Journal of Sociology & Social Welfare*, 37(2), pp. 35–61.

Carayannis, E. and Campbell, D. (2009). 'Mode 3' and 'Quadruple Helix': Toward a 21st Century Fractal Innovation Ecosystem. *International Journal of Technology Management*, 46(3/4), pp. 201–234. DOI: 10.1504/IJTM.2009.023374.

Castells, M. (2000). *The Rise of the Network Society: The Information Age: Economy, Society and Culture* (Volume 1, 2nd revised edition). Oxford: Blackwell.

Chambers, S. (2003). Deliberative Democratic Theory. *Annual Review of Political Science*, 6(1), pp. 307–326.

Chilvers, J. (2008). Deliberating Competence: Theoretical and Practitioner Perspectives on Effective Participatory Appraisal Practice. *Science, Technology & Human Values*, 33(3), pp. 421–451.

Committee on Institutional Cooperation (2005). Engaged Scholarship: A Resource Guide. Available at: www.research2.ecu.edu/Documents/Carnegie/Engagement%20 Scholarship.pdf [5 Oct 2017].

Cook, P. S. (2014). Institutional Frameworks and Terms of Reference: The Public Discussion on Clinical Xenotransplantation in Australia. *Science and Public Policy*, 41(5), pp. 673–684.

Craig, S. C., Niemi, R. G. and Silver, G. E. (1990). Political Efficacy and Trust: A Report on the NES Pilot Study Items. *Political Behavior*, 12(3), pp. 289–314.

d'Andrea, L. (2016). Toolkit Design Document, Deliverable 4.1 of the PE2020 Project. Available at: https://pe2020.eu/wp-content/uploads/2014/02/D4.1-FINAL. pdf [27 Sept 2017].

d'Andrea, L. and Caiati, G. (2016). Toolkit on Public Engagement with Science. Available at: https://toolkit.pe2020.eu/ [24 Aug 2017].

Decker, M. and Ladikas, M. (2010). *Bridges between Science, Society and Policy: Technology Assessment between Methods and Impacts*. Berlin: Springer.

Delli Carpini, M. Cook, F. L., et al. (2004). Public Deliberation, Discursive Participation, and Citizen Engagement: A Review of the Empirical Literature. *Annual Review of Political Science*, 7(1), pp. 315–344.

Dietz, T. and Stern, P. C. (eds.) (2008). *Public Participation in Environmental Assessment and Decision Making*. Washington, DC: The National Research Council.

Dryzek, J. S. (2000). *Deliberative Democracy and Beyond: Liberals, Critics, Contestations*. New York: Oxford University Press.

Dryzek, J. S. (2009). Democratization as Deliberative Capacity Building. *Comparative Political Studies*, 42(11), pp. 1379–1402.

Dryzek, J. S. (2010). *Foundations and Frontiers of Deliberative Governance*. New York: OUP.

Einsiedel, E., Jelsøe, E. and Breck, T. (2001). Publics at the Technology Table: The Consensus Conference in Denmark, Canada, and Australia. *Public Understanding of Science*, 10(1), pp. 83–98.

Elson, R. (2014). Third Wave, Third Sector: A Comparative Provincial Analysis of the Governance of Third Sector Relations. *Canadian Public Administration*, 57(4), pp. 527–547.

European Commission (2008). *Report on the Science in Society Session, Public Engagement in Science*. Proceedings of the Portuguese Presidency Conference 'The Future of Science and Technology in Europe' Lisbon, 8–10 October 2007. Available at: https://ec.europa.eu/research/swafs/pdf/pub_other/public-engagement-081002_en.pdf [12 Oct 2017].

European Commission (2009). Challenging Futures of Science in Society – Emerging Trends and Cutting-Edge Issues. Available at: https://ec.europa.eu/research/science-society/document_library/pdf_06/the-masis-report_en.pdf [27 Sept 2017].

European Commission (2015a). Open Innovation, Open Science, Open to the World. Available at: http://europa.eu/rapid/press-release_SPEECH-15-5243_en.htm [24 Aug 2017].

European Commission (2015b). *Indicators for Promoting and Monitoring Responsible Research and Innovation*. Report from the Expert Group on Policy Indicators for Responsible Research and Innovation, Luxembourg, Publications Office of the European Union.

European Commission (n.d.a). Responsible Research & Innovation. Available at: https://ec.europa.eu/programmes/horizon2020/en/h2020-section/responsible-research-innovation [24 Aug 2017].

European Commission (n.d.b). Societal Challenges. Available at: https://ec.europa.eu/programmes/horizon2020/en/h2020-section/societal-challenges [22 Aug 2017].

Felt, U. and Fochler, M. (2010). Machineries for Making Publics: Inscribing and De-Scribing Publics in Public Engagement. *Minerva*, 48(3), pp. 319–338.

Fiorino, D. J. (1990). Citizen Participation and Environmental Risk: A Survey of Institutional Mechanisms. *Science, Technology and Human Values*, 15(2), pp. 226–243.

Forester, J. (1989). *Planning in the Face of Power*. Berkeley, Los Angeles and London: University of California Press.

Funtowicz, S. and Ravetz, J. (2003). Post-Normal Science. *Online Encyclopedia of Ecological Economics.* Available at: http://isecoeco.org/pdf/pstnormsc.pdf [27 Sept 2017].

Gaskell, G. and Bauer, M. W. (eds.) (2001). *Biotechnology 1996–2000: The Years of Controversy.* London: Science Museum, pp. 96–115.

Gastil, J. and Levine, P. (2005). *The Deliberative Democracy Handbook: Strategies for Effective Civic Engagement in the Twenty-First Century.* San Francisco, CA: Jossey-Bass.

Georghiou, L. and Keenan, M. (2006). Evaluation of National Foresight Activities: Assessing Rationale, Process and Impact. *Technological Forecasting and Social Change,* 73(7), pp. 761–777.

Gibbons, M. (1999). Science's New Social Contract with Society. *Nature,* 402, pp. C81–C84.

Gibbons, M., Limoges, C., Nowotny, H., Schwartzman, S., Scott, P. and Trow, M. (1994). *The New Production of Knowledge: The Dynamics of Science and Research in Contemporary Societies.* London: Sage Publications.

Giddens, A. (1991). *Modernity and Self-Identity: Self and Society in the Late Modern Age.* Stanford: Stanford University Press.

Gieryn, T. F. (1983). Boundary-Work and the Demarcation of Science from Non-Science: Strains and Interests in Professional Ideologies of Scientists. *American Sociological Review,* 48(6), pp. 781–795.

Godet, M. and Roubelat, F. (1996). Creating the Future: The Use and Misuse of Scenarios. *Long Range Planning,* 29(2), pp. 164–171.

Goldschmidt, R. Renn, O., et al. (2008). *European Citizens' Consultations Project: Final Evaluation Report.* Stuttgart: Institut für Sozialwissenschaften.

Goldschmidt, R., Tomblin, D. and Rask, M. (2015). The Role of Gender in Global Citizen Deliberation. In: M. Rask and R. Worthington, eds., *Governing Biodiversity through Democratic Deliberation.* London and New York: Routledge, pp. 130–151.

Goodin, R. E. and Dryzek, J. S. (2006). Deliberative Impacts: The Macro-Political Uptake of Mini-Publics. *Politics & Society,* 34(2), pp. 219–244.

Grönlund, K., Bächtiger, A. and Setälä, M. (eds.) (2014). *Deliberative Mini-Publics: Involving Citizens in the Democratic Process.* Colchester: ECPR Press.

Guldbransen, L. H. (2014). Dynamic Governance Interactions: Evolutionary Effects of State Responses to Non-State Certification Programs. *Regulation & Governance,* 8(1), pp. 74–92.

Hessels, L., van Lente, H. and Smits, R. (2009). In Search of Relevance: The Changing Contract between Science and Society. *Science and Public Policy,* 36(5), pp. 387–401.

High Education Funding Council of England (2007). HEFCE News Bridging the Gap between Higher Education and the Public. In: A. Hart, S. Northmore and C. Gerhardt, eds. (2009), *Briefing Paper: Auditing, Benchmarking and Evaluating Public Engagement.* Available at: https://pdfs.semanticscholar.org/8dbe/660ba40 cfc56c72fb6da52a9c17b0447598d.pdf [5 Oct 2017].

Howe, J. (2008). *Crowdsourcing: How the Power of the Crowd Is Driving the Future of Business.* New York: Crown Publishing Group.

Hyysalo, S., Jensen, T. E. and Oudshoorn, N. (eds.) (2016). *The New Production of Users: Changing Innovation Collectives and Involvement Strategies*. New York and London: Routledge.

IAP2 (2007). IAP2's Public Participation Spectrum. Available at: www.iap2.org. au/Tenant/C0000004/00000001/files/IAP2_Public_Participation_Spectrum.pdf [27 Sept 2017].

Irwin, A. (2001). Constructing the Scientific Citizen: Science and Democracy in the Biosciences. *Public Understanding of Science*, 10(1), pp. 1–18.

Jacobi, A., Klüver, L. and Rask, M. (2011). CIVISTI D3.3 Final Project Report. Available at: www.civisti.org/files/images/Civisti_Final_Report.pdf [27 Sept 2017].

Joly, P. B. and Kaufmann, A. (2008). Lost in Translation? The Need for 'Upstream Engagement' with Nanotechnology on Trial. *Science as Culture*, 17(3), pp. 225–247.

Kies, R. and Nanz, P. (eds.) (2013). *Is Europe Listening to Us: Successes and Failures of EU Citizen Consultations*. Farnham and Burlington: Ashgate.

Klein, J. T. (2004). Prospects for Transdisciplinarity. *Futures*, 36(4), pp. 515–526.

Knowlton, L. W. and Phillips, C. C. (2013). *The Logic Model Guidebook: Better Strategies for Great Results*. Los Angeles, London, New Delhi, Singapore and Washington, DC: Sage Publications.

Kuhlmann, S. and Rip, A. (2014). The Challenge of Addressing Grand Challenges. Available at: https://ec.europa.eu/research/innovation-union/pdf/expert-groups/ The_challenge_of_addressing_Grand_Challenges.pdf [27 Sept 2017].

Levidow, L. (1998). Democratizing Technology – or Technologizing Democracy? Regulating Agricultural Biotechnology in Europe. *Technology in Society*, 20(2), pp. 211–226.

Leydesdorff, L. and Etzkowitz, H. (1998). The Triple Helix as a Model for Innovation Studies. *Science and Public Policy*, 25(3), pp. 195–203. DOI: https://doi.org/10.1093/spp/25.3.195.

Lindblom, C. (1959). The Science of 'Muddling through'. *Public Administration Review*, 19, pp. 79–88.

Lord, C. and Tamvaki, D. (2013). The Politics of Justification? Applying the 'Discourse Quality Index' to the Study of the European Parliament. *European Political Science Review*, 5(1), pp. 27–54.

Lyotard, J.-F. (1984). *The Postmodern Condition*. Manchester: Manchester University Press.

Maassen, P. (2017). The University's Governance Paradox. *Higher Education Quarterly*, 71, pp. 290–298. DOI: 10.1111/hequ.12125.

Mačiukaitė-Žvinienė, S., Tauginienė, L., Rask, M., Mejlgaard, N., Ravn, T. and d'Andrea, L. (2014). Public Engagement Innovations for Horizon 2020: A Refined Typology of PE Tools and Instruments, D2.1. Available at: www.vm.vu. lt/uploads/pdf/D2-1-_PE2020_submission-1.pdf [26 Sept 2017].

Mäenpää, P. and Faehnle, M. (2015). *Avoin, joukkoistava ja aktivismia hyödyntävä kaupunki ('Open, Crowdsourcing and Active City', in Finnish Only)*. Presentation at the R&D day of the Finnish Institute for Deliberative Democracy, 28 October 2015. Available at: www.slideshare.net/Deliberatiivisendemokratianinstituutti/ avoin-joukkoistava-aktivismia-hydyntv-kaupunki [26 Sept 2017].

Mallery, C., Ganachari, D., Fernandez, J., Smeeding, L., Robinson, S., Moon, M., Lavallee, D. and Siegel, J. (2012). *Innovative Methods in Stakeholder Engagement: An Environmental Scan*. Rockville: AHRQ Publication. Available at: www.research gate.net/publication/257497251_PHP5_Innovative_Methods_for_Stakeholder_ Engagement_An_Environmental_Scan [26 Sept 2017].

Mazzucato, M. (2015). *The Entrepreneurial State: Debunking Public vs. Private Sector Myths*. London and New York: Anthem Press.

Mejlgaard, N., Bloch, C., Degn, L., Ravn, T. and Nielsen, M. W. (2012). *Monitoring Policy and Research Activities on Science in Society in Europe* (MASIS). Final Synthesis Report. Available at: https://ec.europa.eu/research/science-society/ document_library/pdf_06/monitoring-policy-research-activities-on-sis_en.pdf [26 Sept 2017].

Mejlgaard, N. and Ravn, T. (eds.) (2015). Public Engagement Innovations – Catalogue of PE Initiatives, D1.2. Available at: https://pe2020.eu/wp-content/uploads/2014/02/ Public_Engagement_Innovations_H2020-2.pdf [26 Sept 2017].

Miah, A. (2017). Nanoethics, Science Communication, and a Fourth Model for Public Engagement. *Nanoethics*, 11(2), pp. 139–152. DOI: 10.1007/s11569-017-0302-9.

National Co-Ordinating Centre for Public Engagement (2017). What Is Public Engagement? Available at: www.publicengagement.ac.uk/explore-it/what-public-engagement [5 Oct 2017].

Neo, B. S. and Chen, G. (2007). *Dynamic Governance: Embedding Culture, Capabilities and Change in Singapore*. Singapore: World Scientific Publishing.

Nicolescu, B. (2002). *Manifesto of Transdisciplinarity*. New York: State University of New York Press.

Nowotny, H., Scott, P. and Gibbons, M. (2003). Introduction: 'Mode 2' Revisited. *Minerva*, 41(3), pp. 179–194.

OECD (2001). *Citizens as Partners: Information, Consultation and Public Participation in Policy-Making*. Paris: Organisation for Economic Co-Operation and Development, p. 267.

Owen, R., Macnaghten, P. M. and Stilgoe, J. (2012). Responsible Research and Innovation: From Science in Society to Science for Society, with Society. *Science and Public Policy*, 39(6), pp. 751–760.

Pardo, R. and Calvo, F. (2002). Attitudes toward Science among the European Public: A Methodological Analysis. *Public Understanding of Science*, 11(2), pp. 155–195.

Parkinson, J. and Mansbridge, J. (2012). *Deliberative Systems: Deliberative Democracy at the Large Scale*. New York: Cambridge University Press.

PE2020 (2017). PE2020 Public Engagement Innovations Horizon 2020: Research Project of the European Union FP7 Framework Programme. Available at: http:// pe2020.eu/ [29 Aug 2017].

Porter, M. E. (1998). *Competitive Advantage of Nations – with a New Introduction*. Basingstoke, UK: Macmillan.

Raelin, J. A. (2001). Public Reflection as the Basis of Learning. *Management Learning*, 32(1), pp. 11–30.

Rask, M. (2003). The Problem of Citizens' Participation in Finnish Biotechnology Policy. *Science and Public Policy*, 30(6), pp. 441–454.

Rask, M. (2008). Foresight – Balancing between Increasing Variety and Productive Convergence. *Technological Forecasting and Social Change*, 75(8), pp. 1157–1175.

Rask, M. (2013). The Tragedy of Citizen Deliberation – Two Cases of Participatory Technology Assessment. *Technology Analysis and Strategic Management*, 25(1), pp. 39–55.

Rask, M., Bedsted, B., Andersson, E. and Kallio, L. (Forthcoming). Democratic Innovation in Transnational and Global Governance. In: S. Elstub and O. Escobar, eds., *The Handbook of Democratic Innovation and Governance*. Cheltenham, UK and Northampton, MA: Edward Elgar.

Rask, M., Mačiukaitė-Žvinienė, S. and Petrauskiene, J. (2012). Innovations in Public Engagement and Participatory Performance of the Nations. *Science and Public Policy*, 39(6), pp. 710–721.

Rask, M., Mačiukaitė-Žvinienė, S., Tauginienė, L., Dikčius, V., Matschoss, K., Aarrevaara, T. and d'Andrea, L. (2016). Innovative Public Engagement. *A Conceptual Model of Public Engagement in Dynamic and Responsible Governance of Research and Innovation*. Publication D2.2 of the PE2020 Project. Available at: https://pe2020.eu/wp-content/uploads/2016/05/Innovative-Public-Engagement-FINAL.pdf [26 Sept 2017].

Rask, M. and Worthington, R. (eds.) (2015). *Governing Biodiversity through Democratic Deliberation*. New York and London: Routledge.

Rask, M., Worthington, R. and Lammi, M. (eds.) (2012). *Citizen Participation in Global Environmental Governance*. New York and London: Routledge.

Ravn, T. and Mejlgaard, N. (eds.) (2015). Public Engagement Innovations – Catalogue of PE Initiatives, D1.2. Available at: www.vm.vu.lt/uploads/pdf/Public_Engage ment_Innovations_H2020-2.pdf [26 Sept 2017].

Ravn, T., Mejlgaard, N. and Rask, M. (2014). Public Engagement Innovations for Horizon 2020: Inventory of PE Mechanisms and Initiatives D1.1. Available at: www.vm.vu.lt/uploads/pdf/PE2020-FINAL-D.1.1-report.pdf [26 Sept 2017].

Regenberg, A. 2010. Tweeting Science and Ethics: Social Media as a Tool for Constructive Public Engagement. *The American Journal of Bioethics*, 10(5), pp. 30–31.

Renn, O. (2008). *Risk Governance: Coping with Uncertainty in a Complex World*. London and Sterling: Earthscan.

Repo, P., Kaarakainen, M. and Matschoss, K. (2015). *European Research Priorities Based on Citizen Visions*. Report on the CASI Expert Workshop Held in Copenhagen 8.-9.6.2015 (WP 3, Task 3.4). Available at: www.casi2020.eu/library/deliverables/ [26 Sept 2017].

Rip, A. (2003). Constructing Expertise: In a Third Wave of Science Studies? *Social Studies of Science*, 33(3), pp. 419–434.

Ritzer, G., Dean, P. and Jurgenson, N. (2012). The Coming of Age of the Prosumer. *American Behavioral Scientist*, 56(4), pp. 379–398.

Roberts, N. (2000). Wicked Problems and Network Approaches to Resolution. *International Public Management Review*, 1(1), pp. 1–19.

Rogers, E. (1995). *Diffusion of Innovations*. New York: Free Press.

Rosa, H. (2013). *Social Acceleration: A Theory of Modernity*. New York: Columbia University Press.

Rotsztein, B. (2013). Managing Your Social Media Footprint. Available at: www. socialmediatoday.com/content/managing-your-social-media-footprint [22 Aug 2017].

Rowe, G. and Frewer, L. J. (2005). A Typology of Public Engagement Mechanisms. *Science, Technology, & Human Values*, 30(2), pp. 251–290.

Rowe, G., Horlick-Jones, T., Walls, J. and Pidgeon, N. (2005). Difficulties in Evaluating Public Engagement Initiatives: Reflections on an Evaluation of the UK GM 'Nation? Public Debate about Transgenic Crops. *Public Understanding of Science*, 14(4), pp. 331–352.

RRI Tools (n.d.). Welcome to the RRI Toolkit. Available at: www.rri-tools.eu/ [24 Aug 2017].

Sabeti, H. (2009). *The Emerging Fourth Sector: Executive Summary*. Washington: Aspen Institute.

San Román, L., de and Schunz, A. (2017). Understanding European Union Science Diplomacy. *Journal of Common Market Studies*, pp. 1–20. DOI: 10.1111/jcms.12582.

Schuitema, G., Steg, L., and Forward, S. (2010). Explaining differences in acceptability before and acceptance after the implementation of a congestion charge in Stockholm. *Transportation Research Part A: Policy and Practice*, 44(2), 99–109.

Seligman, M. E. and Csikszentmihalyi, M. (2014). *Positive Psychology: An Introduction*. Dordrecht: Springer, pp. 279–298.

Shoemaker, A. (2011). Is There a Crisis in International Learning? The 'Three Freedoms' Paradox. *Cambridge Journal of Education*, 41(1), pp. 67–83.

Smith, G. (2009). *Democratic Innovations: Designing Institutions for Citizen Participation*. Cambridge: Cambridge University Press.

Smits, R. and Kuhlmann, S. (2004). The Rise of Systemic Instruments in Innovation Policy. *International Journal of Foresight and Innovation Policy*, 1(1–2), pp. 4–32.

Steenbergen, M. R., Bächtiger, A., Spörndli, M. and Steiner, J. (2003). Measuring Political Deliberation: A Discourse Quality Index. *Comparative European Politics*, 1(1), pp. 21–48.

Stevenson, H. and Dryzek, J. (2014). *Democratizing Global Climate Governance*. Cambridge and New York: Cambridge University Press.

Sutcliffe, H. (2011). *A Report on Responsible Research & Innovation*. Matter and the European Commission.

TEPSIE (2012). EU Funded Project TEPSIE, the Theoretical, Empirical and Policy Foundations for Building Social Innovation in Europe. Available at: http://cordis.europa.eu/project/rcn/101832_en.html [5 Oct 2017].

Tidd, J., Bessant, J. R. and Pavitt, K. (2001). *Managing Innovation: Integrating Technological, Market and Organizational Change* (2nd edition). Chichester: Wiley.

Väliverronen, E. (2016). *Julkinen tiede* (Only in Finnish). Helsinki: Vastapaino.

Voß, J. P. and Amelung, N. (2016). Innovating Public Participation Methods: Technoscientization and Reflexive Engagement. *Social Studies of Science*, 46(5), pp. 749–772.

von Schomberg, R. (2013). A Vision of Responsible Innovation. In: R. Owen, M. Heintz and J. Bessant, eds., *Responsible Innovation*. London: John Wiley.

Warburton, D. (2011). *Evaluation of Sciencewise-ERC*. Didcot: Sciencewise.

Wellcome Trust (2015). Evaluating Public Engagement in the Wellcome Trust's UK Centres. Available at: https://wellcome.ac.uk/sites/default/files/wtp059889_0.pdf [26 Sept 2017].

Williams, C. C. (2002). Harnessing Voluntary Work: A Fourth Sector Approach. *Policy Studies*, 23(3), pp. 247–260.

Wilsdon, J. and Willis, R. (2004). See-through Science: Why public engagement needs to move upstream. London: Demos.

Wong, J. (2015). 'Mini-Publics', Competence and Reliable Decisions. In: M. Rask and R. Worthington, eds. (2015), *Governing Biodiversity through Democratic Deliberation*. New York and London: Routledge, pp. 235–248.

Ziman, J. (1996). Post-Academic Science: Constructing Knowledge with Networks and Norms. *Science Studies*, 9(1), pp. 67–80.

Index

Page numbers in italics indicate figures and page numbers in bold indicate tables.
Boxes and notes are indicated by page numbers followed by *b* and *n* respectively.

132   *Index*

For Product Safety Concerns and Information please contact our
EU representative GPSR@taylorandfrancis.com Taylor & Francis
Verlag GmbH, Kaufingerstraße 24, 80331 München, Germany